16.99

Radical Theatre

CLASSICAL INTER/FACES

Also available

RADICAL THEATRE
Greek Tragedy and the
Modern World

Rush Rehm

Duckworth

First published in 2003 by
Gerald Duckworth & Co. Ltd.
61 Frith Street, London W1D 3JL
Tel: 020 7434 4242
Fax: 020 7434 4420
Email: inquiries@duckworth-publishers.co.uk
www.ducknet.co.uk

A catalogue record for this book is available
from the British Library

ISBN 0 7156 2916 6

Typeset by Ray Davies
Printed in Great Britain by
Biddles Ltd, *www.biddles.co.uk*

Contents

A Note to the Reader

When referring to the tragedies, I have used the OCT editions:

Aeschylus, ed. Denys Page (Oxford 1972)
Sophocles, eds H. Lloyd-Jones and N.G. Wilson (Oxford 1990)
Euripides, ed. J. Diggle, vol. I repr. with corr. (Oxford 1989); vol. II
  repr. with corr. (Oxford 1986); vol. III (Oxford 1994).

Translations are my own, unless otherwise noted.

Abbreviations for Greek authors and texts follow Liddell-Scott-Jones, *A Greek-English Lexicon,* and for scholarly journals, *L'Année Philologique* (founded by J. Marouzeau, Paris) and the *American Journal of Archaeology.* In the English spelling of Greek words, I follow common usage, but I have tried to respect original spelling in quotations. The references in the notes limited to author, year, and page number are keyed to the entries in the Bibliography, where full publication information can be found. Portions of Chapter 1 appear in expanded form in *The Play of Space: Spatial Transformation in Greek Tragedy* (Princeton 2002), and a section of Chapter 2 appears in '*Supplices,* the Satyr-Play – Charles Mee's *Big Love',* *American Journal of Philology* 123 (2002) 111-18. I am grateful to the publishers for permission to incorporate those passages here.

I would like to thank Ron Davies for his technical help with the ms; Herman Altena, Edith Hall and Richard Beacham for responding to specific queries with speed and grace; series editors Paul Cartledge and Susanna Morton Braund for their astute editorial comments, which have improved the book greatly; and Andrea Nightingale for making it all better. *¡Hasta la victoria!*

Introduction

Timely Thoughts

I do not know what meaning classical scholarship may have for our time except in being 'unseasonable' – that is, contrary to our time, and yet with an influence on it for the benefit, it may be hoped, of a future time.

Friedrich Nietzsche[1]

This book aims to recapture the radical nature of Greek tragedy, and to suggest how the contemporary theatre might engage with the world's oldest dramatic form. I use the term 'radical' with its etymology in mind – from the Latin *radix*, 'root', suggesting that Attic tragedy provides a foundation or source for later theatrical activity, and as such can offer sustenance for contemporary performance. But 'radical' also points to something politically dangerous, capable of challenging and undermining accepted practice. Approaching Greek tragedy as a radical source may help us remember what we have forgotten about the theatre, and also point toward some timely innovations.

Let us begin with the fundamental philosophical move, as Socrates might advise, asking the 'what is it?' question of theatre and performance. Contemporary responses to that question have displaced the first term with the second, and the results constitute the burgeoning field of performance studies. A short seven years ago, in her introduction to *Performance and Cultural Politics*, Elin Diamond noted that 'performance discourse, and its new theoretical partner "performativity", are dominating critical discussion almost to the point of stupefaction'.[2] The 'almost' in her judgement seems pre-Noachic, given the flood of studies after hers in which performance provides the subject or the interpretive frame, or both.

Through the sometimes murky waters of this theoretical current one glimpses a distinction between 'performativity' and 'perform-

9

ance'. The first term amounts to a claim that concepts like race, gender, class, status, identity and self have no essence on their own, but come into being only when realized by the second term, a specific 'performance'. Performativity does double duty, however, not only emphasizing the contingent, constructed nature of human experience, but also providing the system of regulatory norms governing (or sanctioning) any given performance, determining what actually can appear in a culture at a particular time. A performance instantiates the performativity of the relevant category, calling it into its temporary, contingent, and evanescent being.[3]

In contemporary literature on performance, the 'what is it?' question turns inexorably on itself, chasing its tail down a möbius-strip of endless iterations. By doing something (almost anything, it turns out), the doer 'performs' his or her 'performativity', demonstrating that he or she emerges only by and through such performances, which draw on and echo (sometimes with distortion) the previous performances which make up self, culture, and society.[4] But, of course, the 'his' and 'her' that do these performances are themselves unstable categories (in this case, of gender), defined and conditioned by *their* own performativity. Without pursuing the argument, we recognize the potentially fatal flaws of tautology and infinite regress, not to mention the distance we have come from commonsense assumptions about the world to which theatrical performances might refer.

The explanation for the popularity of performance theory (at least in the academy) lies outside my purview, but a brief sketch of its intellectual pedigree will help us better understand how ancient views of performance differ from those currently in vogue.[5] Among many points of origin, let us mention three early twentieth-century influences before turning to contemporary thinkers. Freud's notion of a human psyche with hidden depths, divided against itself, and at odds with its surroundings has done much to destabilize notions of personal identity, opening the possibility that the self is constructed through a series of dramatic encounters. Freud's 'discoveries' remain unverified (and unverifiable), but the world of science to which they aspire – with propositions testable by replicable experiment – also has contributed to the decentring at the heart of performance studies. Einstein's theory of relativity (where frame of reference determines observation) and Heisenberg's uncertainty principle (where sub-atomic observation compromises what is observed, so that one can measure a particle's momentum or location, but never both at once) have proved surprisingly influential. Literary and cultural theorists have misinterpreted Einstein and Heisenberg, using their formula-tions to conclude (in bald terms) that 'everything is relative' and 'everything is uncertain', which makes a nonsense of the science and mathematics behind the propositions which they invoke.[6]

A third foundational influence on performance theory involves another misappropriation, this time from the field of linguistics. Saussure's notion of the arbitrary relationship between sign and signifier – e.g., the word 'tree' has nothing treelike about it, only the language convention that it refers to a big wooden plant – has been used by literary critics to suggest a tear in the fabric of being. Ignoring language universals, Chomsky's generative grammar, and Saussure himself, some deconstructionists have detected a gap be-tween word and world so fundamental as to undermine the claims of Western philosophy, the idea of rationality, the assumption of caus-ality and temporal sequence, and even the possibility of communication. All such propositions generate a series of endless (and endlessly futile) substitutions, until there is nothing 'outside the text', no 'there' there.[7]

Selectively exploited and recast, these early twentieth-century ideas feed later theories whose synthesis constitutes the basis of performance studies. Important here is the work of sociologists like Erving Goffman, whose major titles – *The Presentation of Self in Everyday Life* (1959) and *Frame Analysis* (1974) – suggest the basic idea: self-dramatization within a series of socially constructed frames (or games, in Eric Berne's popular study of role-playing, *Games People Play*, 1964). From the philosophy of language, J.L. Austin (*How To Do Things With Words*, 1962) introduced the notion of 'performative utterances', a speech-act that does not simply express an attitude or make an assertion but effectively *does* or *accomplishes* something (a couple saying 'I do' at their marriage ceremony, for example). In *Speech Acts: An Essay in the Philosophy of Language* (1969), John Searle expands and complicates Austin's argument, but resists the claim (popular among performance theorists) that any-thing said by anyone in any context – a character in a play, for example – has performative results. Most of us would agree that a field commander shouting 'Charge' at the battle of Waterloo makes a performative utterance with real consequences, but does the actor playing Uncle Teddy in Joseph Kesselring's *Arsenic and Old Lace*, who utters the same command? Common sense suggests an important difference between the battlefield and the theatre, if not for performance theorists, then at least for the audience, who usually want to leave the theatre alive.[8]

Contemporary views on performance also reflect the influence of cultural anthropology and theories of cultural formation. Van Gennep's division of rites of passage (such as initiation or marriage) into a tripartite scheme of physical separation, a liminal period 'betwixt and between', and social reintegration has had a major impact on performance studies. Victor Turner has applied and adapted Van Gennep's pattern to other 'social dramas', and Richard Schechner has approached performance (whether in ritual, theatre, or everyday life) as 'restored behaviour'.[9] Under these influences, cultural historians and performance theorists have turned increasingly to study para-theatrical events – from royal parades to wrestling matches, from political spectacles to department store window-dressing, from motorcycle rallies to slave-auctions – contributing to the so-called 'cultural turn' in the humanities championed by Frederic Jameson, among others.[10]

Finally, anti-essentialist, 'constructivist' notions of the body, gender, race, and ethnicity have found a home – or at least a house – in contemporary performance theory.[11] The permeable boundaries of performativity offer theoretical space for the various acts by which racial and sexual identities are formed and reformed. Here, 'performance' becomes a basic category of being, or rather of coming into being, with its own paradoxical ontology.

Reflecting the deconstructionist onslaught against the 'metaphysics of presence', postmodern antipathy for the universalist claims of the Enlightenment, and the pressures of academic publication, scholars have turned 'performance' and 'performativity' into catch-all terms, as in Richard Schechner's 'What is Performance Studies Anyway?':

Are there any limits to performativity? Is there anything outside the purview of performance studies? ... The acceptance of the performative as a category of theory as well as a fact of behavior has made it increasingly difficult to sustain the distinction between appearances and facts, surfaces and depths, illusions and substances. Reality is constructed through and through, from its many surfaces or aspects down through its multiple depths. The subjects of performance studies are both what is performance and the performative – and the myriad contact points and overlaps, tensions and loose spots, separating and connecting these two categories.[12]

Under the expanding umbrella of performance studies, the lived world offers various 'theatrical sites' for 'staging' or 'acting out' a myriad of cultural practices that constitute things, ideas, identities, genders, races and selves, and then – by sleight-of-hand, it seems – deconstitute them, even as they come into being.

If the above description approximates the current 'what is it' of performance (i.e. what *isn't* it?), what about contemporary understanding of the theatre? Even as theatrical metaphors permeate academic discourse, the stage *per se* – understood as a place for artistic enactments like Greek tragedy – has lost much of its power and significance. What can the theatre offer a performative world but a pale version of everyday scenes that go on all around it, reminding us that we are constituted by nothing but fictions?[13] In performance studies, the theatre gives way to its derivative term 'theory', particularly the theory that all that matters is performed, and only performance really matters.[14]

In a sense performance studies offers a version of artistic representation where the fallacy of imitative form operates without restraint. Because the stage metaphor *is* reality, or at least the reigning explanation for it, onstage dramas flow noiselessly into those offstage. It is not that what happens in the theatre fools us into mistaking it for something else. On the contrary, for the enlightened critic sceptically attuned to theatricalized reality, the distinctions between the world and stage simply don't matter.[15]

Let us leave contemporary thinking and move back to the classical world, asking the 'what was it?' question of theatre and performance. The first word gives us little trouble: 'theatre' is a Greek word (*theatron*) for the place where spectators (*theatai*) gathered to watch (*theasthai*) a theatrical spectacle (*theama*). In fifth-century Athens, *theatron* invariably refers to the theatre as a place, although the related words for spectator, the act of watching, and what one sees are not theatre-bound. Perhaps that helps to explain why we find no classical Greek reference to the 'theatre of life', or any comparisons of the world to a stage, a trope that proved popular in Renaissance discussions of history and memory, in the Spanish Golden Age, and in Elizabethan and Jacobean England.[16]

We are on more difficult terrain with 'performance', a term for which the ancient Greeks had no single equivalent. In *Performance Culture and Ancient Democracy*, Simon Goldhill harnesses four Greek terms: *agôn* (contest, competition), *epideixis* (a display or demonstration, usually involving public speaking), *schêma* (bodily gesture, carriage, posture, or form), and *theôria* (spectating). These categories reflect a growing interest among classicists in performance studies, where – as noted above – almost anything proves to be 'performative'. Goldhill and Osborne's volume, for example, treats both theatrical and non-theatrical performances, including festival processions, public oratory, philosophical dialogues, and vase painting.[17]

When labelling classical Athens a 'performance culture', we point to overlapping areas of public activity – law courts, the assembly, symposia, the gymnasia, the theatre, and so on – that involved performers and audiences shaping and enacting their idea of the city. We can profit from Greek theatre by keeping this political context firmly in mind. However, it appears that the 'performance culture' of democratic Athens had no trouble distinguishing the stage world from that outside the theatre, and saw no advantage in blurring the practical and ontological differences between the two. We might learn more – both politically and artistically – from the Athenians' institution of the theatre if we followed their lead and resisted viewing tragedy as yet another performance in a world constituted by 'performativity'.

The closest Greek term for 'performance' emerges in ancient discussions of performances themselves (choral poetry, epic, drama), namely *mimêsis*, usually translated 'imitation'. This rendering is accurate enough, if we insist on the mimetic activity implicit in the

English word. We imitate others by taking on their gestures, voice, inflection, mannerisms, clothing, behaviour. However, modern uses of 'imitation' tend to undervalue the action involved; 'imitation crystal', for example, indicates a fake, rather than the act of its manufacture. 'Performance' offers a more comprehensive translation of *mimêsis*, understood as 'enacting', 'impersonating' (without necessarily implying deception or counterfeit), 'acting out', 'acting like', or (in the case of objects) 'being like'. That is, *mimêsis* and its cognates suggest an embodied presentation of somebody or something not otherwise present, which in its manifestation emulates (at least descriptively) that person, behaviour, or thing.

Cognates of *mimêsis* occur three times in Euripides' tragedy *Heracles*, providing a brief compendium of fifth-century usage. Heracles' wife Megara captures the essence of the idea, when she chooses to act as her husband would if he faced the same deadly circumstances: 'I must not reject acting [or "performing", *mimêma*] like my husband' (*HF* 294). In this instance, Heracles provides a model of bravery that Megara can emulate. Later in the play the goddess Hera drives Heracles mad, and he attacks his own sons: 'raising his wooden club like [*mimêma*] a blacksmith forging iron, he brought it down on the boy's blonde head, smashing the skull' (992-4). Here, *mimêsis* involves a comparison between two anomalous events, whose juxtaposition likens the everyday action of a blacksmith pounding his anvil to the deathblow a father deals his son. Once restored to sanity, the hero contemplates his horrific crimes and imagines the punishment that awaits him: 'I will act out a likeness [*ekmimêsomai*] of Ixion, bound in chains to his turning wheel' (1297-8). Here, a prior (mythical) event offers an image or model for Heracles' future. As the first to shed kindred blood, Ixion provides the paradigm of crime and punishment that all subsequent filicides 'imitate', paying a similar price for a similar crime.[18]

These interrelated meanings of *mimêsis* encompass the general sense of the term in early Greek texts.[19] The earliest in-depth exploration of *mimêsis* occurs famously in Plato, who, as Nehamas notes, insists on its total heteronomy: 'As the products of *mimêsis* are images of real things, so the practice of *mimêsis* is the image of a real practice [i.e. the real activity of making real things, not their imitations]'.[20] Gradually the use of *mimêsis* expands to include representation not only by performers (actors, singers, dancers), but also by those who depict or fashion inanimate images of the world (painters, sculptors, architects). But I will use the term in its earlier, more restricted sense, meaning 'embodied performances that act out, act like, or emulate people and things (real or fictional), their behaviour, and their activities, all of which exist (really or in principle) before the performance begins'. Performance in this sense does not constitute the real world; it represents it.

This view of mimetic representation reflects the prevalence and popularity of oral poetry, drama, dance, and musical performance in ancient Greek society. We tend to forget that music accompanied athletic training and competitions, rituals (sacrifice, weddings, funerals, initiations) and feasting. The Delian and Pythian Games and the Panathenaia (the Athenian counterpart to the great panhellenic festivals) held contests for singers, musicians and choruses, as well as for athletes, and the Panathenaia also included contests for rhapsodes.[21] These performers offered a sequence of solo recitations of the great epic stories (particularly from Homer): the war at Troy and the troubled homecomings (*nostoi*) of the heroes; the expedition of the Seven against Thebes; the stories of Heracles; and other tales of the gods and their interactions with mortals. In Homer's *Iliad*, 60% of the lines represent the direct speech of a given character, making the rhapsode less a poetic narrator than an actor, speaking the words of otherwise absent characters and so bringing them to life.[22]

Scholars have argued persuasively that the inclusion of rhapsodic competitions at the Panathenaia (Athens' major civic festival) in the sixth century played a crucial role in creating the new performance genre of tragedy. It is true that Aristotle in *Poetics* identifies the separation of the chorus-leader from the chorus in the dithyramb – a choral genre of narrative poetry dedicated to Dionysus – as a key moment in the birth of drama. However, Aristotle also finds the generic seeds of Greek tragedy and comedy in Homeric epic, particularly in the poem's frequent shifts from straight narration to dramatization, when the characters take on their own voice and speak for themselves.[23]

We see the narrative, story-telling impulse basic to Greek tragedy in set speeches by named characters, in Messenger reports of offstage action, and in passages of lyric narration by the Chorus. The impor-

16

tance of conveying the story constitutes a key legacy of the ancient theatre, one that much contemporary theatrical practice has abandoned in favour of pastiche, visual imagery, non-linear montage, a preference for display over explanation, and for the personal over the social or political. These undercurrents are not absent from Greek tragedy, but when present they tend to serve the narrative, helping to distinguish it from previous versions of the myth.

In this context let us consider the often-voiced accusation that Aristotle's *Poetics* originates an anti-performance prejudice that resurfaces in subsequent writing on the theatre.[24] After all, Aristotle claims that the effect of tragedy can arise from reading ('the force of tragedy can be felt even without benefit of public performance and actors'); he argues that plot – not production – is the 'heart and soul, as it were, of tragedy'; and he shows little respect for the visual aspects of theatrical performance.[25] We should recall, however, that the vast majority of ancient Greeks were illiterate; for them, reading did not mean a private act carried out in silence, but rather a public act of being read aloud to, a mini-performance in itself. Moreover, *Poetics* deals expressly with the composition (*poeisis*, 'making') of dramas, what we would call playwriting. Aristotle rightly privileges the author of tragedies, who in the fifth century also served as director, composer, choreographer, and sometimes lead actor. In Aristotle's time, however, that situation no longer obtained. Fourth-century tragic productions featured spectacular effects, star turns (including wholesale actor interpolations), and the transposition or removal of choruses. Aristotle's insistence that the effects of tragedy can arise from reading may reflect his reaction to the production excesses of his day.[26]

Taking Aristotle's good meaning, *Radical Theatre* returns time and again to the challenges of engaging the original form of ancient tragedy as best we can, rather than altering the material to fit contemporary tastes. Form refers to the structuring principles through which each play delivers its 'deep content', to adapt a phrase of architect St John Wilson.[27] Embedded not only in the text, tragic form also is bound up in the performance practices of ancient Athens, a subject we will address in Chapter 1, 'Theatre, Artifice, Environment'. Not surprisingly, the Athenians had a myth to illustrate the problem of recalcitrant form. They told of a villain Procrustes, who

17

feigned hospitality and invited wayfarers to stay for the night. Then, using a hammer and axe, he pounded out or hacked up his victims until they exactly fitted the bed he had prepared for them. It would be disappointing if the place of Greek tragedy in the contemporary theatre involved Procrustes-like operations on the unsuspecting guest, inserting missing elements or removing offending excess, killing the 'deep content' in the process.

Chapter 2, 'Theatre and Fear', juxtaposes the impulse for drama and the impulse for fear and flight, what the Greeks called *phobos*. As a genre Greek tragedy confronts the horror behind appearances, exposing the blindness of intellect and the destructiveness of passion, showing human beings as vulnerable, cruel, violent, brave, foolish, compassionate. Time and again tragic characters conquer their fear and act at the edge of the abyss. This is a situation with which we can identify. Without exaggeration, we face the palpable destruction of our natural environment;[28] the exploitative juggernaut of trans-national capitalism; the ethical challenge of genetic engineering; the militarization of nations and proliferation of deadly weapons; the widening gap between rich and poor; the assault on traditional societies; and a crisis of meaning for many individuals and communities. In the face of such abysmal fears, many find themselves numbed into passive acceptance, bought off by the mirage of escape, or driven to extraneous activities that steer clear of the real problems. By its very honesty, Greek tragedy can encourage us to face those harsher truths. Specific plays offer theatrical beacons to help us navigate our own cultural phobias: the *Oresteia* and *Prometheus Bound* link progress and destruction; the two *Electra*'s show the compulsions to revenge and the costs of resistance; *Hecuba* pairs cruelty and perseverance, innocence and violence; *Heracles* exposes the randomness of events, and the human effort to make headway all the same. In both form and content, these tragedies suggest useful perspectives on current predicaments, encouraging us to imagine – and even work – our way through them.

As discussed above, performance studies has joined zealously in the postmodern disparagement of personal agency – given the performativity of unstable, impermanent, and multiple selves, *whose* agency could it be anyway? Perhaps Greek tragedy can suggest ways out of this conundrum as well. Chapter 3, 'The Agency of Fate, the

Fate of Agency', explores the close relationship in tragedy between human freedom and constraint. The cry *ti drasô* ('What shall I do?') – which Jean-Pierre Vernant calls *the* tragic question – marks crucial moments in several Greek plays, suggesting that human choice is part and parcel of the workings of fate.[29]

Chapter 4, 'Theatre and Ideology', moves from personal agency to the larger problem of how tragedy dramatizes the ideology of the Athenian *polis* and its empire. Issues of slavery, oppression, the status of women, militarism, violence, the abuse of language, and the representation of the 'other' provide specific areas for comparison between ancient and modern theatre and thought. Contemporary performance theory aims to reveal the encoded rules that govern performativity and suggest how a given performance might circumvent them. Options include refusing to enter any discursive field [!]; offering a performance so fleet and ephemeral that it cannot serve a pre-existing narrative (like a falling snowflake that dissipates before joining the snow that blankets the ground); or presenting a performance that encourages variations, emphasizing that the reproduction implicit in any performance (of gender, race, identity, or the theatre) is never exact.[30]

In the third case, performance resembles a genetic playground, where mutations happen in the very process of replication, without the conscious choice of any single gene. Benighted humans who think they can change the rules or opt out of the game forget that they merely are 'performing' an alternative role or 'staging' resistance. In the least sanguine of these scenarios, a wilful gesture of dissent only reconfirms the system, for the very fact of its emergence ties it inextricably to previous narratives that have, already, 'scripted' it. Even the most intentionally radical performances – so the story goes – run the risk of supporting the status quo, constituting yet another product for reproductive consumption.[31] Perhaps Greek tragedy can open up a different space, its bracing otherness evoking a more expansive view of the prospects before us. Even in the state-sponsored performances of fifth-century Athens, the replication of ideology 'never did run smooth'. Must it now, or in the theatre of the future?

Chapter 5, 'Theatre and Time', speculates on the relationship between performance and temporality, an appropriate terminus for a book that tries to understand the past and future of Greek tragedy in mutually illuminating terms. For the Greeks, humans were *ephêmeroi*, 'creatures of a day', a fair description of human beings generally, but even more apt for those involved in live theatre, among the most ephemeral of human activities. Thinking about the theatre and time recalls the danger of accepting performance and performativity as if they constituted reality. Famine victims may 'perform' their hunger for a television camera, but this says more about the media than about starving people. Prisoners may assume roles and act them out, but the states that execute them are playing for keeps. The victims of torture don't 'stage' their agony. The 1991 Gulf War may have seemed to Americans like a video game, and to postmodern theorists like a virtual campaign, but not to the 200,000 Iraqi conscripts mowed down in the 'turkey shoot in the desert', nor to the hundreds of thousands of civilians who have died since because of the US-driven sanctions.[32] Real-life experiences help us see the banality of the performance metaphor when it is spread so thin and covers so much, occluding the fact that time – insofar as it is concerned with us – does have a stop. That fact extends from individual deaths to the extinction of entire human cultures and biological species.

The miracle of Greek tragedy's survival – literally as texts transcribed over centuries, in some cases by scribes who could not understand what they were copying – calls us to celebrate a happy accident of history, and also to engage wholeheartedly in what that accident demands from us. Requiring moment-to-moment realization in a *mimêsis* not co-extensive with reality, Greek tragedy reminds us that humans live real lives (the only ones we have) and die real deaths, no matter how hard we try to deny it. Those hard truths provide the inspiration for tragic performance, and suggest simply and directly why this ancient form of theatre might be particularly timely now.

1

Theatre, Artifice, Environment

Light dawns gradually over the whole.
Ludwig Wittgenstein

The Greek word *theatron* means a place where spectators watch a performance, and in classical Athens the most important such place was the theatre of Dionysus, the venue for which almost all surviving Greek tragedies and comedies were written. For the last five hundred years, however, the word 'theatre' generally has meant a walled and roofed building that allows artists to exercise heightened aesthetic control by cutting out the natural environment around them. Using available technologies of lighting, sound, stage machinery and theatre construction, theatres since the Renaissance have become temples to artifice. Even innovators who seek to recover the unalloyed thing itself – Antonin Artaud in *Le Théâtre et son Double*, Jerzy Grotowski in *Towards a Poor Theater* – usually imagine and utilise a structured indoor performance space for their work.[1] Contemporary interest in theatre as virtual reality – employing video, surround sound, holography, computer effects, and other 'smart' technologies – points to a future of ever more 'wired' spaces.

In cases where the contemporary theatre resists the indoors, it still fends off the natural world. So-called 'environmental' staging frequently involves moving the audience around and through indoor spaces, and when 'found environments' are used or site-specific works developed, artists usually rig the spaces for lights and sound to alter their mundane character. Contemporary productions of old plays do occur in outdoor theatres – Shakespeare in the Park in Manhattan, Greek tragedies and comedies in the fourth-century theatre at Epidauros – but they generally take place at night, under lights, with electronically reproduced music and other amplified sound. We have

21

grown accustomed to attending theatre in places that focus attention on the performance at the expense of the natural world.

Such was not the case in the fifth-century theatre of Dionysus in Athens, where the wooden façade (*skênê*) behind the orchestra limited the view beyond the theatre for only a small portion of the audience. From various vantage points, those gathered on the south slope of the Acropolis could see an array of natural and built phenomena stretching to the horizon. Later Greek theatres, and those built by the Romans, did close off the vista by constructing high stone backdrops; they also blocked off the side entrances connecting the orchestra with the outside world, effectively walling the theatre up while leaving it open to the sky. Eventually, roofed theatres became the norm, improving the acoustic qualities of the space and funnelling audience attention even more onto the stage, preparing for what eventually would become the indoor theatres that most of us know.

Wycherley suggests how fifth-century Athens incorporated the surrounding environment into the theatrical landscape:

> The Greeks liked to take the main structure of their theatres ready made from nature ... [T]he normal method of building on whatever happened to be the most convenient hillside meant that the theatre had no recognized place; and in fact it is found in many different parts of the city and suburbs ... The Dionysus theatre was curiously linked with the surrounding parts of the city, and was less a self-contained unit than most theatres.[2]

The fact that the Athenians' theatre shut out neither the natural nor the civic environment speaks volumes about their theatrical 'aesthetic' – aggressively public, part of the ongoing life of the city, subject to the forces of nature (the major dramatic festival took place in early spring, the lesser ones in winter), played against a backdrop of the *polis*, acted out on a beaten earth *orchestra*, with the land, sea, and sky beyond. Roland Barthes observes that, in such performances, 'the spectator's immersion in the complex polyphony of the open air (shifting sun, rising wind, flying birds, noises of the city) restores to the drama the singularity of the event'.[3] The kind of reproducible artistic control offered by the modern stage never occurred to those who originally prepared and performed Greek tragedy. Instead of

22

artifice and illusion, they dealt with the elements – both in the play's subject matter and in its performance.

What kind of dramatic material could stand up to such an expansive, open-air setting? Without romanticizing the ancient Athenians (who responded minimally to such stirrings), it may be said that they invented a theatrical form that was deeply grounded, exceedingly confident, simple in plot, archetypal in character, strict in form, vast in emotion, cosmic in purview, Athenian in spirit. Dance, music, masked performers, and ensemble choruses arrested the audience's attention, as did the legendary, larger-than-life characters who interacted face-to-face ('mask-to-mask') even with the gods, who often appeared on the tragic stage. Drawing on popular myth, tragedy enacted old stories against a backdrop of nature and the city, their progress measured by the unfolding narrative as the sun crossed the sky.

Given Greece's Mediterranean blessings, it is hardly surprising that the sun and sky feature in its poetry and drama. Nonetheless, it is remarkable how frequently tragic characters and choruses address the sun, 'the god foremost of all the gods' (Sophocles *Oedipus Tyrannus* 660-1). Tragedies and satyr-plays often make reference to sunlight or the dawn near their outset, effectively merging the mythical world with that of the audience (the fictional and the real sun being one and the same).[4] Consider Alcestis' farewell hymn to the light of life that she is leaving:

> O Sun, and light of fleeting day,
> and clouds that race across the whirling sky...
> Hades draws near.
> Shadowy night creeps over my eyes....
> Children, delight in this light you can see.
> Euripides *Alcestis* 244-5, 268-9, 271

To lose the light of the sun meant to live no more, and Hades (*a-idês*) was the place for the 'invisible' or 'unseen'. Alcestis' death becomes more immediate and palpable by virtue of her appeal to the sun that both she and the audience can see.[5]

In Euripides' *Bacchae*, Pentheus describes his descent into the Dionysiac world by crying out, 'Ah look, I seem to be seeing two suns, and a double Thebes ...' (*Ba.* 918-19). After Pentheus' death, Cadmus uses the sky overhead to bring his daughter Agave *out* of her Dionysiac madness:

> *Cadmus*: First, look up at the high sky overhead.
> *Agave*: I see it. But why do you want me to look there?
> *Cadmus*: Does it seem the same to you, or has it changed?
> *Agave*: It's brighter than it was before, and clearer.
> ...
> *Cadmus*: Look straight at it [the object in your arms] now. It's a small thing to look.
> *Agave*: No! What do I see? What am I holding in my arms?
> *Cadmus*: Look closely; learn the answer clearly.
> *Agave*: I see the worst of pain, wretch that I am.
> Euripides *Bacchae* 1264-7, 1279-82

Agave discovers that the head she holds in her arms is not a lion's but her own son's. Sun and sky operate as touchstones in a world gone mad, measuring both the extent of the delusion and the means to recover from it, revealing the horrible truth that Agave must come to see. Time and again in tragedy, the illusion of theatrical performance meets the reality of the natural world, reminding the audience of the inescapable context that defines, and enables, any human drama.

At the end of *Medea*, the triumphant heroine appears in the chariot of her grandfather, the sun-god Helios, with the corpses of the children she has killed. Greek poets frequently imagine the sun as a chariot moving across the sky, and Medea's appearance actualizes the image. Euripides' spell-bound Pentheus sees 'two suns' over Thebes, but it is the audience who have this double vision in *Medea*. They see the chariot of Helios carrying Medea, and the real 'chariot of the sun' in the sky, the celestial orb invoked throughout the play to look on, and stop, injustice.[6] Immediately before Medea's filicide, the Chorus make just such an appeal:

> O ... ray of the sun god [Helios] that lights
> all things, look, oh look down on
> this deadly woman, before she turns her
> bloody murderous hands on her own children
> ...

24

1. Theatre, Artifice, Environment

O god-born light, stop this cruel murdering Fury,
take her from the house plagued by vengeful spirits.

Euripides *Medea* 1251-4, 1258-60

The Chorus' wish is fulfilled, but not in the way they hoped. The sun
god does remove Medea from the house, but only *after* she commits
the murder that destroys it. By juxtaposing Helios' chariot with the
real sun, Euripides reminds his audience that Medea is not a natural
force (as many critics claim), but a human who has suffered horribly
and acted worse. In an indoor theatre, her extraordinary final appearance might conjure an apotheosis; in the outdoor theatre of
Dionysus, however, it falls purposefully short. The sun in the sky
does not rescue Medea or save the day. Rather, it shines down on the
perpetrator as she flies off to Athens, bringing her criminal vengeance home to the Athenian audience.

Let us follow Medea, and move from the natural world to the civic
world where the tragic performances took place. From their different
vantage points, the audience looked down over the temple and sanctuary of Dionysus, the city walls, and as many as five city gates.
Visible from the *cavea* were various sanctuaries and temples,
shrines, lawcourts, and private houses of the southern city, the oldest
inhabited part of Athens outside of the Acropolis.[7] Those sitting high
up saw the Ilissos valley and the extension of the city to the south,
including the gymnasium of Kynosarges and the Kallirrhoe spring,
which provided water for the nuptial baths that a bride and groom
took (separately) as part of their wedding ritual; to the east they
viewed the slopes of Mount Hymettos, known for marble quarries
that provided some of the building material for Athens' public monuments; to the south and west appeared the Saronic gulf and, rising
above it, the peak of Prophitis Ilias on the island of Aegina, the site
of the shrine of Zeus Panhellenios, where Athenians sheltered when
the Persians occupied and burned their city in 480. Behind and above
the audience loomed the Acropolis, packed with various cult sites,
most of them dedicated to the goddess Athena.

Given this impressive civic backdrop, it seems surprising that only
four of our surviving 33 tragedies (but every extant Aristophanic
comedy) are set in Attica – most of Aeschylus' *Eumenides* (Acropolis,
Areopagos), Sophocles' *Oedipus at Colonus*, Euripides' *Suppliant*

25

Women (Eleusis) and *The Children of Heracles* (Marathon). However, several tragedies end with protagonists making their way to Athens, including Euripides' *Medea, Heracles, Ion, Iphigenia among the Taurians, Electra,* and *Orestes.* Others evoke Athens and its environs at important moments (Aeschylus' *Persians,* Sophocles' *Ajax,* Euripides' *Trojan Women* and *Hippolytus*). *All* the tragedies employ a skein of references to contemporary political, social, economic, military, religious, and artistic practices, from democratic elections to marriage rituals, from lawcourt rhetoric to political debate, from official religious cults to the Peloponnesian War, from public monuments to earlier tragedies performed at the theatre of Dionysus. This anachronistic weave tied the old myths (generally set in Troy, Argos, Thebes or Corinth) to the contemporary world of the (mainly) Athenian audience.

Consider, for example, Aeschylus' *Persians,* unique among extant tragedies in dramatizing an historical event, the Persian expedition against Greece and its defeat by the Athenian navy at Salamis. Twice Xerxes' invading forces sacked and burned Athens, and the rubble was still visible from the theatre when the *Persians* premiered less than a decade later, in 472. Remarkably, the play is set in Persia and told from the Persian perspective. The sounds ringing out from the Athenian orchestra are the laments of the defeated foe, not the triumphal cries of the Greeks. Although the play manipulates the realities of history and of Persia in pro-Athenian ways, it nonetheless demands that the audience sympathize with the Asian enemy.

Much of the drama involves the Persians invoking the distant war in Greece, and the devastation inflicted by the Athenians. With the arrival of the defeated Xerxes at the end of the play, however, Athens seems to drop out. Twice in the last seven lines (1070, 1074), as the Chorus follow Xerxes out of the theatre, they sing 'Ah! Ah! the Persian earth is hard to tread'. But the Persians elders who walk away are – of course – Athenian performers in disguise, crossing the beaten earth of their own city's *orchestra.* They have enacted a theatrical 'invasion' of Persians, but this time the foreigners have come to mourn, not conquer. As the theatre space merges with the real world, the rubble outside the theatre suggests a background of common loss rather than partisan triumph. The openness of the

Athenian theatre to the natural and civic environment worked a sympathetic magic that other theatres must struggle to achieve.

Time and again tragedy draws together the natural world and the built environment of the *polis*, forging a deep connection between art and audience, between fiction and reality, between culture and nature. Let us look briefly at how that extraordinary union operates in plays set in the city of Thebes, considered by many scholars now to represent the 'dramatically other' in opposition to a glorified Athens.[8] The opening lines of the Chorus in *Antigone* provide a good starting point:

> Hail the sun! Brightest
> of all that ever dawned
> on the seven gates of Thebes,
> great eye of golden day,
> sending light across
> the rippling waters of Dirce ...
>   Sophocles *Antigone* 100-5

The audience who watched the Theban Chorus praise the dawn also saw the sun overhead, the southern city gates of Athens below the sanctuary of Dionysus, and the reflected light off the Ilissos river to the east, analogous Athenian elements to those in the choral song. In terms of *Antigone*'s plot, the morning sun heralds Thebes' victory over Argos, the successful expulsion of disaster from the city. However, it also brings to light a new disaster, emanating from the corpse of Polyneices, exposed and rotting as the day progresses (*Ant*. 410-12). Antigone appears over the body 'when the bright circle/ of the sun stood in the middle of the heavens/ warming us with its heat' (415-17). As the tragedy moves towards its climax, Teiresias warns Creon that he faces his own disaster 'before the racing sun completes many laps' (1064-5). The sun signals key moments in the mythic world of the play, even as it marks the passage of time during the performance.

The acknowledgement of natural elements, and the parallels between the Thebes and Athens, *break down* the differences that separate the two cities. *Antigone* does not simply relate the further misadventures of the Oedipus-clan caught in a specifically The-

27

banesque cycle of self-destruction. Rather, it tells a cautionary tale about political tyranny and resistance, about the essential role of women in the family and the city, about the proper relationship between the living and the dead. It deals as much with fifth-century Athens as it does with a mythic Thebes, and that transference arises naturally from the way that text and environment came together in performance at the theatre of Dionysus.

Similarly, the fact that Sophocles' *Oedipus Tyrannus* opens with two scenes focussed on a plague makes it unlikely that the Athenian audience saw the Thebes of the play as some 'negative other'. By having two successive groups enter from outside the theatre describing the epidemic, Sophocles conjoined the mythic Thebes of the drama with the plague-ridden Athens of his own day,[9] suffering from 'that most calamitous and awful visitation', as Thucydides puts it. The historian describes the epidemic's effect ('heavily did it weigh on the Athenians, death raging within the city and devastation without'), made worse by the fact that it never seemed to end: 'The plague a second time attacked the Athenians .... The second visit lasted no less than a year, the first having lasted two; and nothing distressed the Athenians and reduced their power more than this.'[10]

If the audience identified with the plagued city of Oedipus, then the Theban setting did not signal an anti-Athens, but an imaginative extension of the city of Athena, suggested by the early reference to the 'two temples of Pallas' (*Pallados diplois/ naois* 20-1), where suppliants gathered to pray for release from disaster. Although Thebes possessed several temples to the goddess, as Jebb observes, 'It was enough for Sophocles that his Athenian hearers would think of ... the shrines of the Polias and the Parthenos above them on the acropolis'.[11] In the same vein, the Teiresias scene and Oedipus' subsequent encounter with Creon take on aspects of an Athenian trial, and the theatre comes to resemble a fifth-century lawcourt, or *dikastêrion*.[12] Far from highlighting its difference from fifth-century Athens, Sophocles emphasizes Thebes' commmonality with the contemporary world of the audience.

The same principle applies to Aeschylus' *Seven Against Thebes*, where the Athenian recollection of the effects of the Persian invasion – still visible from the theatre, as noted above – receives mythic scope. In this play (performed five years after *Persians*), Thebes is described as 'Greek-speaking and free', one that resists the yoke of slavery (*Sept.* 72-5, 792-4) and fights off invasion by a 'foreign speaking army' (166-70). Havelock suggests that 'language like this recalls the Persian threat, not a situation in which Greek meets Greek as in the Theban story'.[13] The dual dangers of foreign invasion and internal faction allowed the scenic space of Thebes to provide a fictional locus for Athenians to consider their *own* circumstances in 467, when the Persian empire still threatened and Athenian political unity was tested over how to respond.

In *Antiope*, Euripides dramatizes a central foundation myth of Thebes, setting the action at a cave in Eleutherai, a village on the border between Attica and Boeotia that gave the name to the Dionysiac cult (Dionysus Eleuthereus) celebrated at the City Dionysia. Not only was the god's temple visible just below the theatre, but the cult image of Dionysus Eleuthereus was present during the performance of the play.[14] Although most of the text of *Antiope* has been lost, we know that the Chorus consisted of Athenian men, to whom (possibly) Amphion delivers a monody accompanied by a lyre: 'I sing of Aither and Earth the mother of all things.'[15] As this passage suggests, Thebes and Athens – for all their political rivalry – share the bright upper air and the earth from which all living things spring. Rooted in Athens but exposed to the world, the theatre of Dionysus forged powerful links between 'distant' theatrical settings and the actual site of tragic performances.

In dramaturgical terms, the theatre's openness to the environment allowed for arrivals and departures from the distance, via the two side entranceways (*eisodoi*) that visibly linked the orchestra to the world beyond, and also via the *mêchanê* ('machine'), a crane-like device that 'flew' divine figures on and off the roof of the *skênê* building, as at the end of *Medea*. Such comings and goings from afar supplemented the entrances and exits through the central portal in the *skênê* facade, which approximated an upstage centre door in a modern realistic set. However, unlike a standard box set where the door opens *into a room* (with the fourth wall removed), the *skênê* aperture (when used) opened out-of-doors. That is, with very few exceptions, tragic action takes place outside, in a 'public area' in front of a temple, palace, cave or tent. Unaffected by the assumptions of bourgeois drama and theatrical realism, Greek tragedy accommodates arrivals from the distance more easily than most theatrical genres. The beaten earth of the *orchestra* stretches 'naturally' out to Thebes, to Troy, to Persia, to Egypt, to the furthest limits of the known world. Distant characters didn't enter 'from the wings'; they crossed the earth of Attica, and returned from whence they came in the same manner. A similar pedestrian – but by no means mundane – reality applied to the audience, who entered and left the theatre, as far as we can tell, through the same *eisodoi* as the actors.

As noted in the Introduction, modern scholars are fond of pointing out the verbal link between theatre and theory: in ancient Greek, a *theatron* ('theatre') is a place where 'spectators' (*theatai*) 'look' or 'see' (*theasthai*). The related word 'theory' (*theôria*) indicates 'a way of seeing', the set of spectacles (as it were) that one wears when looking at a given phenomenon. By a rather over-zealous declension, some contemporary intellectuals have come to view the theatre as *the* place for theory. However, this etymological link between the two terms leaves out an essential middle step, part of Greek cultural practice that can help us better understand the connection between theatre and thinking. As well as 'looking' or 'beholding', the term *theôria* meant 'a pilgrimage, visitation, or mission', usually of an official or public religious nature. In Aristophanes' *Peace*, for instance, the character Theôria appears as a kind of 'official spectator' attendant on her mistress, Peace. Ancient Greek cities sent a *theôros* (plural *theôroi*) as an 'official representative' to important religious sites (the oracle at Delphi), to panhellenic celebrations (the games at Olympia or Nemea), and to foreign courts and rulers (diplomatic missions, envoys, ambassadors). A *theôros* indicates someone who 'travels in order to witness', a 'visitor' in the Latin root-sense (*videre*) of one who goes 'to see'. Such a traveller is neither a spectator in our sense (someone who sits in front of the television to watch 'spectator sports') nor a 'theorist' (someone who adopts a certain mental attitude in order to think, and then tells us about it).

The operative issue involves how we understand the audience for which tragedy was written. In fifth-century Athens, it seems that people who attended theatrical festivals acted more as unofficial *theôroi* ('envoys who come to see') rather than as simple *theatai* ('spectators'). Going to the theatre resembled other *theôriai*, including pilgrimages to religious sanctuaries, the Eleusinian Mysteries, healing shrines, and so on.¹⁶ Such a 'theoric' pilgrimage included making preparations and departing from home; travelling to a designated area to offer sacrifice, inquire, watch, learn; and returning with something important to report or share. It is in this light that we might understand why Plato opens his *Republic* with Socrates walking back from a religious festival at Piraeus, five miles from the centre of town. Socrates' theory of a utopian society emerges within the context of a theoric visit. As we know from the famous analogy of the cave later in the *Republic*, the philosopher is obliged to *return* to the cave (the world we mistake for real) to share his insight with those who mistake the shadows cast on the wall for reality. Leaving, experiencing, returning, and reporting were part and parcel of whatever 'seeing' took place for Plato's philosopher, and we find a similar process at work in the dramatic festivals of Athens.¹⁷

At the City Dionysia, people came from all over Attica and the Greek world. Although an Athenian festival, its regular occurrence in early spring (when the seas were open for sailing) encouraged a panhellenic audience. The festival offered a kind of license, a holiday from the normal workaday world. Various rituals – most notably a public sacrifice, with meat distributed to Athenian citizens at the city's expense – marked its special nature, as did the dramatic and dithyrambic competitions presented over several days. However, as discussed above, the theatre of Dionysus and the performances themselves exploited the continuity between spectators and performers. They all entered the same space, under the same light; the Choruses consisted of Athenian citizens, who trained for the event but were non-professionals; citizen members of the audience chosen by lot voted on the best production and actor; the Assembly met *in the theatre* after the festival to discuss how things had been run and the city's resources used. Given the nature of ancient performance, the audience did not sink into the passivity we associate with being a spectator. They were active participants, *theôroi* on a theatrical mission.

As I hope is clear, this theatrical *theôria* did not privilege isolated consciousnesses engaged in internal contemplation for its own sake. On the contrary, the public and communal nature of Greek tragedy involved religious, cultural, and political imperatives far removed from our contemporary notion of personal entertainment on the one hand, or 'art for art's sake' (aesthetics as private religion) on the other. This public thrust constitutes one of the most difficult facets of the ancient theatre for moderns to grasp, fed as we are on the importance of individuals and their mental processes, interior musings, and private truths.

Many influences have contributed to our cathexis on the individual, including Enlightenment and Romantic interest in subjectivity, the rise of psychology as a social science, the capitalist ideology of the selfish consumer, the transformation of community-based religious worship into belief in a personal god (with silent prayer, private contrition, and so on). Because it represents human behaviour, the theatre naturally has reflected those changes, both in performance space and in dramatic content. The conventions of theatrical realism, championed in the nineteenth century and still dominant today, allow those in the audience to look in on a basically private world, and to do so without being seen. In effect, such theatre requires the effacing of the audience by focussing all light and attention onstage, the standard arrangement in proscenium-arch theatres.[18]

Although 'realistic' plays frequently take on large issues and themes, the dramatic lens invariably narrows to the vicissitudes of an interior life. In spatial terms, the action moves into the drawing room, dining room, bedroom, kitchen, library, office, pub. Temporally, the plays find their measure in the clock on the mantle, as if the interior scenography structured the passage of time.[19] Kinesthetically, drama becomes increasingly sedentary, abandoning the music and dance central to ancient theatre and substituting in its place the ubiquitous chair, sofa, stool, bench or seat of power. Psychologically, dramatic characters *per se* emerge as the focus of the drama, their personal hopes, anxieties, moods, and idiosyncrasies replacing issues of public moment framed by an objective narrative. Realist dramas generally show individuals caught in a society or social situation that fails to recognize their uniqueness or difference. Realist comedies feature clever characters who celebrate their individuality by defying social convention. To oversimplify, realistic theatre reverses Aristotle's dictum, making character – not plot – 'the soul [*psychê*, "animating force"] of the drama'.[20]

Greek tragedy, on the other hand, appeals to the individual not in his or her uniqueness, but as an essential participant in a social and political community, one that must find its proper place within the constraints of the natural world. Lacking a divine creator outside of creation, the Greeks of the fifth century saw their gods as 'in and of the cosmos' and limited by it. The same applied to humans, as we will discuss in Chapter 3. The famous exhortation carved over the temple of Apollo at Delphi – 'Know yourself' – did not encourage solipsistic self-analysis, as we might think. Rather it urged humans to understand their place as terrestrial mortals in the larger scheme of things.

The aggressively public thrust of Greek tragedy reflects the radical form of government practised by the Athenians, what we would call direct democracy (from *dêmos* and *kratos*, 'people power'). Given the need for informed citizens to govern the *polis*, a general notion of propaedeutic and community-building provided the *raison d'être* for city-sponsored dramatic competitions. Over the past 20 years, scholars have paid renewed attention to the social and political function of Greek tragedy, emphasizing its promotion of civic ideology and its role in defining and moulding the Athenian citizen.

However, the related ideas that tragedy existed only for the male citizens of Athens, and that its civic focus made it parochial, xenophobic, and exclusively Athenian, fail to account for the genre's catholic form and broad appeal. As noted above, the myths at the core of Greek tragedy were panhellenic, and only rarely did the playwrights treat local Athenian stories. The lyric sections (sung and danced by the Chorus) incorporated expressive modes from across the Greek world (hymns, prayers, dirges, paeans). Moreover, the tragedians followed the Greek convention that choral lyric was composed in Doric, meaning that tragic lyric uses a version of the Dorian dialect (mainly from the Peloponnese) rather than the Ionian idiom spoken in Athens. As for dramatic focus, time and again female characters serve as the protagonists, even though Athenian women – like women across the globe, even in recent times – lacked political franchise. So, too, non-Greek characters in tragedy frequently provide the magnet for audience sympathy, challenging any simple notion of the superiority of Athenian male citizens or of Greeks in general, a subject we will return to in Chapter 4, 'Tragedy and Ideology'.

As for tragedy's popular appeal, the audience at the City Dionysia were by no means only Athenian, and frequently non-Athenian playwrights and actors competed and won prizes. Although an invention of Athens, tragedy became extremely popular outside Attica, with theatres sprouting up all over the Greek world. Both Aeschylus and Euripides wrote plays for non-Athenian audiences, in Sicily and Macedonia respectively, and it is there that each playwright died. The export of tragedy beyond Attica has drawn increasing attention from classicists and theatre historians alike, correcting the earlier Athenocentric emphasis.[21]

Returning to the environmental openness and formal eclecticism of Greek tragedy, we recognize an image of inclusivity that current champions of pluralism and multiculturalism should find appealing. Tragic performances privileged no single perspective or point of view; they depended on a collaborative process involving the city and its people, professionals and amateurs, Athenians and non-Athenians, playwrights, performers and musicians. The adaptability of myth, the openness of the theatre, and the flexibility of the Chorus allowed tragedy to range freely across space and time. Characters arrive from offstage, from a distant city, even from Olympus; into the diachronic thrust of the narrative enter past memories, future projections, cyclical temporalities, ritual and mythic timelessness. As a performance genre, tragedy incorporates a variety of 'discourses' – rhetorical speech, forensic argument, political debate, dramatic dialogue, religious hymns, lyric poetry, monody, threnody, choral song, dance – adapted to new uses. Masked actors represented individuals and groups, humans and gods, slaves and kings, males and females, old and young, heroes and outcasts, Greeks and foreigners. Throughout the fifth century, the form of tragedy developed and changed, stretching but never breaking the conventions that allowed it to grow into itself.

Pushed too far, of course, the idea that tragedy represents some contemporary ideal of inclusivity is ludicrous. Ancient Athens was no utopia, and it suffered many of the outrages and committed most of the sins that bedevil other human communities. As a product of the society from which it sprang, tragedy reflected Athenian imperialism, sexism, hypocrisy, intolerance, and a host of other ills. And yet time and again the plays confront and expose these failings, challenging the audience to think them through. For lack of a better term, most Greek tragedies manifest the qualities to which we give the name 'classic' – in particular, a bracing provocation to engage a work's complexity and bring it to life in our own time and place.[22]

Given the original conditions of Greek tragic performance, and the interplay between theatrical artifice and natural environment, how might we approach tragedy now in a way that unlocks its radical potential? If we start with Sophocles' *Electra*, for example, we might ask what we mean by invoking that author and title. According to the anti-positivism popular today, it is a leap of (blind) faith to assume we mean much of anything beyond an appeal to a constructed authority. We know little about Sophocles, nothing of his intentions, and, no matter how hard we try, not all that much about his *Electra*. True, we have some late manuscripts of his tragedy written in Greek, but what do we really know about the original text, much less about the play as manifest in the theatre of late fifth-century Athens? Exercised with sufficient scepticism, interpretative relativism extends from textual readings, metrical schemes, and assignment of lines to the size and constituency of the original audience, the performance style for which the play was written, the nature of the theatre in which it premiered (orchestra shape, presence or absence of raised stage, use of scene painting, etc.), the sound of the musical accompaniment, the quality of choral dance, and so on. Some would scrap the whole project of approaching Greek tragedy *per se* as pointless historicism, a vain effort to track an 'original' that remains at best elusive, and at worst misconceived, the very enterprise built on essentialist nonsense.

Following this line of argument, 'Sophocles' *Electra*' is whatever we want to make of it, the 'it' representing anything from the Greek text to an English adaptation, from a reconstructed staging to a mixed-media event where things Greek, Sophoclean, and original play no part. Such an open-ended attitude – or 'found object' approach, the object being anything we identify as Sophocles' *Electra* – ignores the long tradition of textual editing that aims to arrive at the best Greek text, the work of scholars who go all the way back to the Alexandrians of the third century BCE, and even before. Their painstaking examination of surviving manuscripts and earlier scholarly conjecture tries to determine the version closest to what Sophocles wrote for performance in the late fifth century. The resulting text provides the basis for translation into other languages, which in turn provide the impetus for adaptations of the drama that may abandon the Greek text altogether.

Downplaying efforts at textual reconstruction, anti-positivists also underestimate what scholars have discovered about fifth-century theatre and culture. This research has led to valuable insights into the non-textual aspects of Sophocles' *Electra*, ranging from the details of tragic production in the fifth century to the social and political context of Athens in the decade the play premiered, information relevant to a meaningful engagement with Sophocles' work. Although certainty eludes us on these and other questions, it seems reasonable to use what we know, especially if we want to recover the radical challenges posed by Greek tragedy. Such an effort does not commit us to antiquarianism and the proverbial museum production. As everyone who works in the theatre knows, that way deadness lies. On the other hand, the 'found object' approach that ignores the history and culture that produced Greek tragedy usually results in an artistic 'sausage', stuffed with various elements gathered from the director or adapter's sensibilities that say far more about them than the subject of our inquiry.[23]

Even those dismissive of the value of textual and historical research need some circumscribed idea of Sophocles' *Electra* if they are to talk about different interpretations or productions of the play. To invoke Plato, we need a 'form' of *Electra* to which these interpretations and productions bear some relationship. This basic issue of reference is prior, but related, to that of loyalty to an original text. Do we mean something detailed by 'Sophocles' *Electra*', or are we using the title loosely? For instance, does it matter that we're speaking of Sophocles' *Electra* and not the play of the same title written by Euripides, or the earlier play with a different title (*Choephori*) on the same subject by Aeschylus? Or are we substituting a general sense of the 'story of Electra' for the particular elaborations of Sophocles' tragedy? If *that* is the case, what about the aspects of Sophocles' treatment that differentiate it from other versions – language, plot, character, the placement and subject of choral odes, the dramatic focus? Are they accidental but not essential, interesting but not worth the trouble?

This is precisely the approach taken by the great structuralist anthropologist Claude Lévi-Strauss in analysing the Oedipus' myth.[24] The repeating patterns of the story of the Labdacids replace the artistic specifics of Sophocles' play, a fate that has affected *Oedipus Tyrannus* perhaps more than any other tragedy. Freudians, too, single out a single aspect of the play (patricide/incest), replacing an artistically crafted piece for the theatre with the ubiquitous Oedipal complex. Adaptations of the play, from Voltaire's *Oedipe* to Berkoff's *Greek*, make similar reductions, leaving Sophocles' play more or less unexamined.

At a minimum, some notion of a given Greek tragedy provides a necessary point of *comparison*, against which we can see theatrical productions of the play, evaluate the degree and effect to which they reconstruct, abandon, alter, or manipulate the original (understanding that comparisons demand stability somewhere in the system). As a matter of principle, I believe we learn more from Greek tragedy the more we take it on its own terms, and the less we make it look and sound like something 'written yesterday'. When it premiered in 1924, for example, Eugene O'Neill's *Desire Under the Elms* dealt with the tragedy of misaligned love in a way that spoke to a 1920s American audience, intrigued (as O'Neill was) with Freud and his version of incest and oedipal themes.[25] We might describe the play as a successful adaptation of a Greek myth by a major modern playwright. However, its very comprehensibility avoided the challenges that its model, Euripides' *Hippolytus*, might have posed for the same audience.

Make no mistake – there is nothing wrong or untoward about such adaptations, and we should celebrate good theatre wherever we find it. The Greek tragedians themselves adapted prior myths and, as the century progressed, reworked earlier dramatic versions into their plays. In understanding their work, issues of prior versions help us identify the tragedians' new emphasis and focus, just as the study of Shakespeare's sources concentrates on what Shakespeare did with them, not on the sources themselves. So, too, a study of Eugene O'Neill's *Desire Under the Elms* or *Mourning Becomes Electra* (his post-American Civil War version of Aeschylus' *Oresteia*) understandably will focus on those works *per se*. To reconnect with the radical nature of Greek tragedy, however, we must go beyond popular adaptations and engage with tragedy's differences from our own theatrical forms, aesthetic principles, and sociopolitical organization.

We must grapple with unfamiliar cultural assumptions and the peculiarities of foreign dramatic conventions, in order to see our own society and its artifices from a new perspective.

To reckon how tragedy captured the imaginative and emotional response of its original audience, or to propose contemporary approaches that might replicate that effect, is a daunting task. Although constituting under 3% of the fifth-century tragic corpus, the 33 surviving tragedies/satyr-plays demonstrate sufficient variety to escape most generalizations about the genre. True, many plays concentrate on dynastic triumphs and failures – the royal houses of Thebes, Troy, Argos, Corinth, Athens – which has led some contemporary directors to view them as domestic dramas about dysfunctional families. Such an approach ignores the public nature and impact of that dysfunction, which inevitably goes further and deeper than the idiosyncratic. Some modern productions have the feeling of cosmic soap operas (as if substituting a *Reader's Digest* summary for Wagner's *Ring*), but even a superficial encounter with the Greek text makes such versions seem trivial. The language of tragedy ranges far beyond the personal, domestic, and familial; the dramatic situation in which tragedies are embedded has deep communal roots; and tragic outcomes have profound social, political, moral, and religious implications.

Modern myths, like those of Freud and his followers, suggest another potential starting point for contemporary production, although again we confront the inadequacy of psychological explanations to account for tragedy's scale and compass. Jungian archetypes, useful in identifying basic polarities and discerning psychic patterns, also lack the political and moral imperatives that sustain Greek tragedy. Materialist approaches that emphasize economic and social forces – the foundation of theatrical realism, still the aesthetic model for much Western theatre – have difficulty accounting for the mythic, numinous, and extra-human dimensions which are no less central to the experience of tragedy. Exotic 'world-culture' approaches like that of Ariane Mnouchkine in *Les Atrides* (her version of Euripides' *Iphigenia in Aulis* and Aeschylus' *Oresteia*) suggest the foreignness of the Greek material, restoring dance and movement to centre stage. However, they can strike us as neither fish nor fowl, ripping non-Western theatrical forms from their cultural context, and at the same time abandoning the verbal, forensic, and rational elements that inform the Greek originals. A musical version like Lee Breuer's popular *Gospel at Colonus* can provide a celebratory and spirited experience, but does so by sacrificing the drama and the harsh contours of the myth that give a play like *Oedipus at Colonus* its terrible – and very non-Christian – power.

No formula exists for capturing what Greek tragedy has to offer contemporary theatre. We cannot travel backwards in time, but we can bring the past forward, the basic meaning of our word 'tradition'. Societies that 'conquer' the environment and flee from history (as the United States most certainly does) have all the more need to engage such tradition. Sadly, when that confrontation does happen, we frequently see the radical theatre of the Greeks converted into new cultural products that 'go down easy' (like Charles L. Mee's adaptation of Aeschylus' *Supplices*, entitled *Big Love*), or that simply 'send up' the original (the gay-fantasy *Medea the Musical*, where Medea's and Jason's marital problems turn on their having failed to 'come out'). Such watered-down approaches constitute a failure of the imagination, not a rediscovery of the strange and challenging world of Greek tragedy. We learn nothing except our own superiority to the past, which is – at least in the theatre – something of a lie. Greek tragedy isn't holy, and playwrights, translators, and directors have every right to meet the material creatively, to take risks, to change things, to behave as theatre artists do. But the stakes in tragedy are high, and their roots go deep. This chapter has tried to suggest that we lose the radical potential of Greek tragedy by failing to deal with its rootedness in the natural environment, the public world, and the dramatic text itself.[26]

2

Tragedy and Fear

The Spartans built a temple to *Phobos* [Fear] and worshipped him as a god; the Athenians ... celebrated tragedy.[1]

For a rational human being, the right to be frightened is the most important one left today.

Herbert Marcuse

Greek drama deals with terrifying stories that have stuck to Western consciousness like leeches. Oedipus, the house of Atreus, Troy, Medea – each evokes a shudder, especially when we recall the narrative behind the name. In these (and other) dramas, the ancient audience confronted an extraordinary array of frightening incidents: incest and cannibalism; matricide, patricide, filicide, suicide, even genocide; disease, plague and insanity; rape, torture, cruelty, betrayal; home-lessness and exile; sacrilege, religious pollution and moral break-down; the degradation of slavery, the horrors of war and the terror of imminent death. As Nietzsche asks in *Birth of Tragedy*, what kind of society could give rise to such a genre, one that celebrates such deep, unequivocal and desolating fears?

The Greeks used many words for the terror evoked by such events, but the most common – *phobos* – has a salutary concreteness we should keep in mind. From Homer onward, its principal meaning was something like 'panic flight', the emotional surge that compels men in battle to turn and run away. In Aeschylus' *Seven Against Thebes*, *Phobos* is personified 'Rout', a son of the war-god Ares (*Sept.* 45). One Argive invader has a shield that clangs out 'terror' (*phobos* 386), another flashes flight-provoking fear (*phobos* 498) from his eyes. All the while, 'Terror' (*Phobos* 500) boasts what he will do outside the gates. Fear so infects the city that Eteocles implores the terrified Theban maidens to change their panicked outbursts to a ritual cry of

40

sacrifice, performed to lessen 'the terror [*phobon*] of battle' (270) and lead to victory.[2]

The words *tarbos* ('alarm', 'terror') and *tarbeô* ('I become frightened or alarmed') signal a similar sense of fright. In *Phoenician Women*, Polyneices describes how he walked through Thebes with his sword brandished, 'feeling great fear' (*etarbêsa*) as he moved 'in terror' (*phobon*, Eur. *Pho.* 361). In *Heracles*, the protagonist hunts down his own children, who flee 'terrified with fear' (*tarbountes phobôi*, Eur. *HF* 971). Deianeira worries over the fate of her husband in *Women of Trachis*, starting suddenly from her sleep, 'frightened with terror' (*phobôi … tarbousan*, S. *Trach.* 176).[3]

The word *deos* ('fear', 'alarm') and the related *deima* ('fear'), *deidô* ('I fear'), and *deimainô* ('I am afraid') indicate a comparable emotion. In *Andromache*, the Nurse chastises Hermione for wanting to flee and escape her husband's wrath: 'I do not condone this fear [*deima*] of yours, wherein you fear [*deimaineis*] far too much' (Eur. *Andr.* 868). The Chorus of *Electra* describe the shield of Achilles 'fashioned with emblems of terror [*deimata*] against the land of Troy' (Eur. *El.* 456-7), designed to 'turn the eyes of Hector to flight [*tropaioi*]' (468-9). The word *tropaios*, from which we get 'apotropaic' ('driving away evil'), marks the turning point in a pitched battle, when one group breaks ranks and runs. A *tropaion* (whence our 'trophy') was erected by the victors to mark the spot. Iolaus in *The Children of Heracles* hopes to make Eurystheus 'turn and run' (*tropên*), being 'too much a coward to stand up to the spear' (Eur. *Hcld.* 743-4). In *Antigone*, Creon warns against insubordination that 'shatters the spears of your fellow-fighters/ and puts them to flight [*tropas*]' (S. *Ant.* 674-5). On the verge of murdering her husband in *Agamemnon*, Clytemnestra shouts her triumph like a cry at the 'turning point [*tropêi*] of battle' (A. *Ag.* 1237), transforming her home into a war zone.

Directly or indirectly, these passages invoke fifth-century Greek warfare, all too familiar to original audiences. Armed with spears and shields, soldiers (hoplites) mustered into opposing ranks and met *en masse*, until one side broke and fled for their lives.[4] As Thucydides observes, fear had predictable consequences in every hoplite encounter, for each soldier sought the cover of his neighbour's shield, which might protect the spear-wielding (right) side of his body. Because of this interdependent arrangement, the files of men tended to edge towards the right, as each soldier sought the protection of his neighbour's armour.[5]

We might contrast the emotional and physical responses to such proximate battle with those arising in contemporary warfare, where death tends to be inflicted from a distance. While military planning and technology have vastly increased the destruction of war, they have depersonalized combat by removing combatants from the havoc they wreak. The visceral turmoil of battle takes a backseat to the technological 'efficiency' of surface-to-surface missiles, 'smart' bombs, high-powered ordnance, grenade launchers, automatic weapons, and landmines.[6] It is hard for us to imagine the terror of proximity basic to Greek hoplite battle, which put a premium on forging ahead and, at minimum, standing one's ground. Each hoplite had to master his fear in order to strive for group survival and victory.[7] Although we find Greek words for fear and terror unrelated to battle, we should keep the realities of ancient warfare in mind as we consider the importance of fear in tragedy.

Not surprisingly for so embodied an art, the theatrical vocabulary of terror and dread emphasizes its effects on the body. The verbs *tremô* and *tromeô* ('tremble', 'quake', 'quiver') and related words implicitly link human experience to that of hunted animals, whose corporeal response to fear is all too evident. At the crucial moment in the *Iliad*, when Hector and Achilles finally confront one another before the gates of Troy, 'the shakes' (*tromos*) steal over Hector and he flees 'in terror' (*phobêtheis*), his pursuer Achilles compared to a hawk chasing a dove (*Il.* 22.136-44). The verbs *ptêssô, ptôssô* ('shrink from', 'cower', 'cringe') evoke a cornered rabbit or a trapped dove, and *phrissô* ('shiver', 'shudder') refers to the hair rising on the back of the neck or a chill running down the spine. In *Oedipus Tyrannus*, the hero flees from his (assumed) father in Corinth, 'trembling in fear (*tremôn*) that he might one day kill him', as the oracle predicts (S. *OT* 947-8). Confronting the blind Oedipus, the Chorus turn away, overwhelmed by 'a fearful chill' (*toian phrikên, OT* 1306), just as earlier they suffered the mental effects of terror: 'I am on the rack, my frightened [*phoberan*] thoughts shaking with fear [*deimati pallôn*]' (*OT* 153).

In Euripides' *Ion*, Creusa abandons the child of her rape by Apollo, filled with 'shuddering fears' (*phrikai* 898) at taking so desperate a step. After her miraculous reunion with her son, Creusa still 'trembles with terror' (*phobôi tremô*, 1452) that he might be snatched from her. In *Trojan Women*, Helen emerges brazen and beautiful from the sack of Troy, when she should appear 'in rags, trembling and shuddering in fear [*phrikêi tremousan*]' before the husband she has betrayed (Eur. *Tro.* 1026). Hunting down the killer of Clytemnestra in Aeschylus' *Eumenides*, the Furies find Orestes 'cowering' (*ptôka*) before the cult image of Athena (A. *Eum.* 326), much like the pregnant hare that cowers (*ptaka*) at Aulis before being devoured by the twin eagles in *Agamemnon* (A. *Ag.* 136). Near the end of *Oedipus at Colonus*, as thunder calls Oedipus to his destiny, the Chorus respond: 'Terror [*deima*] spreads to the tips of my hair,/ and my spirit cowers [*eptaxa*]' (S. *OC* 1465-6). By emphasizing these physical reactions, tragedy underlines the continuity between human and animal worlds, even as it suggests the strength of character needed to act in the face of such fear.

In his *Poetics*, Aristotle famously pairs the emotions of terror (*phobos*) and pity (*eleos*), arguing their centrality to the experience of tragedy. Euripides links them in exemplary fashion when the Chorus of *Phoenician Women* express their dismay at Jocasta's efforts to stop the war between her sons:

Alas, alas. Such shuddering,
shuddering horror in my heart,
[*tromeran phrikai/ tromeran phren*]
and through my flesh courses a sense of pity, pity [*eleos eleos*]
for that wretched mother.

Euripides *Phoenician Women* 1284-7

In his *Rhetoric*, Aristotle defines fear as 'pain or disturbance due to imagining some destructive or painful evil ... so near as to be imminent'. This emotion is felt with great force by 'those who believe something is likely to happen to them, at the hands of particular persons, in a particular form, and at a particular time'. Pity bears a symmetrical relationship to fear, representing our affective response to others who find themselves in fearful situations: 'What we fear for ourselves arouses our pity when it happens to others.'[8] According to Aristotle, tragedy evokes our (other-directed) pity when the circumstances facing dramatic characters are the kind that would make us afraid. Similarly, tragedy evokes our (self-directed) fear when we 'see ourselves' in tragic characters and their dilemmas. In Lessing's view, the *phobos* that Aristotle specifies for tragedy involves the fear 'that we ourselves might become objects of pity .... [T]his fear is compassion referred back to ourselves.'[9]

Aristotle believes that tragedy arouses our pity and fear in a manner and context that give us pleasure. Without rehearsing the multiplicity of responses to this paradox,[10] most of us would agree that tragedy involves an emotional transference of some sort. As an audience, we may not approve of particular dramatic characters, for example, but without an emotional response to their situation, it is hard for us to sustain interest in their story. Aristotle believes that such emotional reactions provide the basis for a deeper change within the audience: 'The emotions ... for example ... fear ... are those things that cause people to change their judgements.'[11] Greek tragedy features characters in fearful and pitiful circumstances, whose emotional responses affect the audience and help account for whatever tragic pleasure follows. With this in mind, let us examine some of the significant fears expressed in Greek tragedy, and then explore parallels between these tragic phobias and our own.

A lyric passage in Sophocles' *Oedipus at Colonus* expresses an attitude towards the exigencies of life typical of tragedy:

> Whoever wants a greater share
> of life, not keeping to a moderate
> portion, has it skewed.
> ...
> Not to be born wins the prize,
> by all accounts. But once you come into being,
> to go back from where you came
> as fast as possible – that comes second.
> When you are young, empty-headed
> and easy with life,
> what painful blows lie
> ahead? What crushing grief won't find you?
> Murder, civil strife, discord, war, envy!
> And last place? That goes to

> damnable old age, powerless, friendless,
> alone, where evils of every shape
> are your only neighbours.
>> *Oedipus at Colonus* 1211-13, 1224-38[12]

To live is to fear the future, except for the young, who remain blind to the dreadful things that lie ahead. And if humans survive those terrors, old age awaits with its desperations and disappointments.

Comparable statements from other sources in the fifth century indicate that Sophocles' Chorus, far from life-hating curmudgeons, express a common view. According to the atomist Democritus, for example, 'Old age is perfect disfigurement, it has everything and lacks everything'. From a prospective point of view, Democritus observes that 'the old man has been young, but it is uncertain whether the young man will reach old age; a good accomplished is better than one to come, which is still uncertain'.[13] The potential for disaster within a context of inevitable change and probable disappointment characterizes a central aspect of Greek popular thought.

This bleak picture uncannily anticipates the Duke's speech in Shakespeare's *Measure for Measure*, delivered to the condemned Claudio:

> Be absolute for death. Either death or life
> Shall thereby be the sweeter. Reason thus with life:
> If I do lose thee, I lose a thing
> That none but fools would keep ...
> ... Thou hast nor youth nor age,
> But as it were an after-dinner's sleep,
> Dreaming on both, for all thy blessed youth
> Becomes as aged, and doth beg the alms
> Of palsied eld; and, when thou art old and rich,
> Thou hast neither heat, affection, limb, nor beauty,
> To make thy riches pleasant. What's yet in this
> That bears the name of life? Yet in this life
> Lie hid more thousand deaths; yet death we fear,
> That makes these odds all even.
>> *Measure for Measure* 3.1.5-8, 32-41

We can point to other passages in tragedy that celebrate joy, happiness, prosperity, friendship, love, the thrill of living. Nonetheless, the idea that human life unfolds as a degradation recurs throughout Greek tragedy, and it is not surprising that tragic characters and Choruses fear the worst.

An important check on this dreadful negativity lies in the fact that the afterlife offered few attractions for the Greeks. A dim, ghost-like existence in Hades didn't hold a candle to life in the sun, as Homer's Achilles tells Odysseus in the underworld: 'Better to work as a serf on another's land/ than rule over the exhausted dead' (*Odyssey* 11.489-91). Another adage of Democritus captures the sentiment, anticipating the conclusion of Hamlet's 'to be or not to be' soliloquy two millennia later: 'The unwise hate their life, yet want to live for fear of Hades.'[14] Disdain and fear for the underworld meant that suicide in Greek tragedy (and in Greek culture generally) signalled hopelessness and shame (Antigone, Haimon, Eurydice, Deianeira, Jocasta, Ajax), and not the calm, rational conclusion that death offers a logical way out.[15] As Aristotle puts it, 'Fear makes humans deliberate, whereas no one deliberates when things are hopeless' (*Rhetoric* 5.15). Like other forms of death for the Greeks, suicide constitutes the end of deliberation, not its triumph.

Camus once said that suicide was the only interesting philosophical question, a claim that the Greek tragedians would not have understood. Far more intriguing to them was the challenge of acting in the face of fear, as Aeschylus' *Prometheus Bound* demonstrates.[16] According to the myth, the human race proved so disappointing that Zeus wanted to destroy it and try again. Out of pity, Prometheus saved humans by providing them with fire and other means to brighten their dark world: language, mathematics, rational thought, social organization, agriculture, housing, society, and – not the least – blind hopes that keep them from foreseeing their own deaths (*PV* 248-51). Prometheus suffers terribly for his rebellion; indeed, the play opens with a scene of his torture, as Zeus' henchmen drive a stake through his chest and bind him to the rock.

Although pinioned and brutalized, the immortal Prometheus boasts that he knows no fear: 'Why should I be afraid, for my fate is not to die?' (*PV* 933). However, the physical anguish he suffers and will face in the future – his ever-regenerating liver eaten by an eagle day after day for hundreds of years (1020-5) – undermines his claim to stoic equanimity. Hearing the sound of birds (perhaps presaging his future torment), Prometheus cries out 'Everything that comes my way makes me fearful [*phoberon*]'. The Chorus of Oceanids, the gull-like sea nymphs who have startled him, respond 'Don't be afraid' (*mêden phobêthêis*, 127-8), but they themselves are terrified. In a transference of emotion typical of tragedy, Prometheus strikes *them* with terror:

> A fearful [*phobera*] mist shot out at my eyes
> filling them with tears
> when I saw your body
> withering away on this rock. (144-7)

> Piercing terror [*phobos*] speeds through my heart,
> and I feel fear [*dedia*] at your fate. (181-2)

> I shudder with fright [*phrissô*] to look at you,
> broken by boundless torture,
> and yet you don't fear [*tromeôn*] Zeus ... (540-2)

Although the Chorus try to persuade him to give in to Zeus, Prometheus holds firm, oozing sarcasm at the god's lackey, Hermes:

> Am I shaking? Maybe a little?
> Cowering [*hupoptêssein*] before you young gods? (959-60)

> Don't fool yourself, thinking that I
> will grow soft, emasculated by fear [*phobêtheis*] (1002-3)

However, at the apocalyptic end of the play, when the earth opens to swallow him, Prometheus cries out at 'this onslaught from Zeus,/ piling terror [*phobon*] upon me ...' (1089-90).

Prometheus' fluctuations between fear and defiance never weaken his resolve to guard his foreknowledge from Zeus. The lord of Olympus is destined for a marriage that might engender a son stronger than the father, the mythic archetype that shaped Zeus' own accession to power when he overthrew his father Cronos. As a result, Zeus exhibits a typical tyrant's paranoia (224-5) and desperation (947-52), fearing his own fall from authority. Tyrannical rulers in other tragedies react similarly when they feel their power threatened: Aegisthus in *Agamemnon*, Creon in *Antigone*, Lycus in *Heracles*, Pentheus in *Bacchae*. In Euripides' *Electra*, Aegisthus marries his step-daughter Electra to an impoverished farmer, 'fearing [*deisas*] that a noble marriage might breed/ a son to avenge Agamemnon's murder' (Eur. *El.* 22-3). Theseus in Euripides' *Suppliant Women* describes the despotic tyrant as 'fearing [*dedoikôs*] for his rule', ready to kill any potential rival, and treating the state's resources (whether material or human) as his personal possessions (Eur. *Su.* 446). The paranoia of power gets ample treatment in tragedy, but nowhere more so than in *Prometheus Bound*, which deals with the most powerful ruler of all, Olympian Zeus.

Combining stubbornness, pride, foresight, and courage, Prometheus does not bend to Zeus' threats. Even more remarkable is the stance of the normally timid Oceanids, who choose to remain with Prometheus through the apocalyptic finale. Earlier, fear ruled their reactions to their tortured relative, and also to Io, Zeus' human victim in the play. But at the crucial moment, when Hermes warns them to leave or suffer Prometheus' fate, the Oceanids choose to stay. They conquer both terror and cowardice (*kakotêta* 1066) in an act of fellow-feeling, as the earth opens and swallows them along with Prometheus. Their pity – the other-directed correlative to self-regarding *phobos* – proves sufficient to overcome their fear of imminent destruction. We find similar, if less fully realized, resistance to political tyranny in the Chorus' stance against Clytemnestra and Aegisthus at the end of *Agamemnon* and throughout *Choephori*; in the reaction of the Chorus (albeit impotent old men) to Lycus in *Heracles*; and in the undercurrent of support for Antigone against Creon's decree that gradually emerges in *Antigone*.

As for Zeus in *Prometheus Bound*, his fear admits an insecurity that tragedy frequently ascribes to politics and political rule generally. This uncertainty extends beyond the paranoid psychology of tyrants with authoritarian personalities; it reflects the fears and insecurities of government *per se*, particularly those associated with radical democracy. Instability and fear were as basic to the life of the Athenian *polis* as they were to tragic protagonists. We see this most clearly in *Oedipus Tyrannus*, a play that juxtaposes the personal phobias of Laius, Jocasta, and Oedipus (stemming from the devastating prophecy from Delphi) with more generic fears associated with political rule.[17]

Let us deal with the individual fears first. Laius exposed his son in order to avoid the 'terrible event he feared [*to deinon houphobeito*]', the oracle's pronouncement that he would die at the hands of his own child (*OT* 721-2). In a mirror image of his father, Oedipus follows a similar path of fear (*phobôi* 974) based on the oracle that he will kill his father and sleep with his mother. Although Polybus' death in Corinth ostensibly removes the possibility of patricide, Oedipus remains hemmed in by terror: 'How can I not still fear intercourse with my mother?' Jocasta answers his question with another question: 'Why should people be afraid [*phoboit*] when what actually happens/ rules their lives?' (976-8). Jocasta offers cold comfort; both she and Oedipus – like most characters in Greek tragedy – do *not* know what really is happening, and that fact *should* fill them with fear.[18]

But the play also deals with the more impersonal fears that affect those who govern the *polis*. Renouncing any interest in replacing Oedipus as king of Thebes, Creon insists on the advantages of remaining second-in-command:

> … Why would anyone want
> to rule in fear [*phoboisi*] rather than have
> the benefits of power and sleep unafraid [*atreston*]?
> …
> Now I get everything from you without fear [*phobou*],
> but if I myself ruled, I would have to do much against the grain.
> (*OT* 584-6, 590-1)[19]

Creon manifests the fear intrinsic to governing at the end of the play, when he assumes power and cautiously consults Delphi *a second time* before sending Oedipus into exile (1436-45). The radical change in Oedipus' fortunes makes any ruler recognize how insecure power, position, and privilege really are.

Aeschylus' *Suppliant Women* also brings together personal and political fears, emphasizing their impact on the community at large. Fleeing from Egypt, the daughters of Danaus seek refuge at the altars of Argos, 'sitting like a flock of doves/ in fear [*phobôi*] of their hawk relatives' (223-4). The predatory image (recalling the Homeric

49

simile applied to Achilles and Hector noted above) refers to the Chorus' Egyptian cousins, who want to force them into marriage. The Danaids supplicate the Argive leader Pelasgus, who 'shudders [*pephrika*] to see the shrines shrouded [with suppliant boughs]' (346), and expresses great fear for his city: 'I am at sea, and fear [*phobos*] seizes my heart/ whether to act or not, and suffer the consequences' (379-80). When the women threaten suicide at the altars rather than marry their cousins, Pelasgus takes up their cause as suppliants sacred to Zeus: 'Fear [*phobos*] of him [Zeus] is supreme among mortals' (479). By admitting total powerlessness, a suppliant assumed a sacred aura, attracting the protection of Zeus, the strongest god (outside of Hades). The terror that drove the foreign women to Argos causes anxiety in the city's ruler, which he subordinates to the greater fear of offending Zeus by dishonouring his suppliants. Pelasgus argues the Danaids' case before the Argive assembly, where the air 'shuddered [*ephrixen*] with raised right hands' voting to grant them asylum (607-8). The citizens' democratic response answers Pelasgus' earlier fears, when he 'shuddered' (*pephrika* 346) at the sight of the suppliants and the dangers they represent.

The beleaguered women, however, remain possessed by terror (*phobôi* 513), which increases (*phoboumai* 734) with the arrival of their Egyptian cousins. 'Terror and dread' (*periphobon … tarbos* 736) overwhelm them and consume them 'with fear' (*deimati* 738). The subsequent (lost) plays of the trilogy tell how the Egyptians defeat the Argives in battle and force the women to submit to marriage. With no choice but to acquiesce, the Danaids take revenge by murdering their husbands on their wedding night, all except Hypermestra, who spares Lynkeus.[20] Conquering their earlier fears, which had led them to consider suicide, the women answer forced submission to marriage with calculated slaughter. In the Danaid trilogy, fear builds on itself until it breaks, unleashing deadly violence against the original instigators of that fear.

In his adaptation of *Supplices* entitled *Big Love* (mentioned briefly at the end of Chapter 1), American playwright Charles Mee follows Aeschylus' plot, but fear plays little part in the proceedings. The asylum seekers are wealthy young Greek women fleeing arranged marriages with their Greek-American cousins. The hospitable Piero (the Italian villa-owning Pelasgus figure) has no taste for a fight, and no community materializes that might feel threatened (the play develops no sense of an 'Argos'). As a result, the stakes of *Big Love* never rise to the tragic dilemma of the original. Whatever transformation Mee's asylum-seekers undergo, it has less to do with fear than with an elite sense of outrage that things won't go exactly as they want. This releases wonderful comic energy and theatrical fun, but none of the emotional depth of Aeschylus' original.

The Danaids flee their pursuers in terror, and their desperation has its parallels today, where women face arranged marriages, enforced submission, rape, domestic violence and institutional forms of political and economic oppression.[21] Moreover, in *Suppliant Women*, the Egyptian Danaids refer to themselves as dark-skinned (A. *Su.* 277-90, 496-8, 719-20, 745), distinguished from the Argives whom they supplicate for help. This important detail suggests a troubling correspondence between Aeschylus' world and our own, involving the politicized racism that underlies refugee policy in countries like the United States.

To take one example, between 1981 and 1991, the US Coast Guard intercepted 24,559 black Haitians who were fleeing a brutal military dictatorship armed and supported by the United States (first Baby Doc Duvalier, then the junta that overthrew Aristide). All but 11 were sent back home to Haiti to suffer repression, imprisonment, torture, and worse. In the same period, the US Coast Guard picked up 75,000 Cubans (mostly white), *every one* of whom received asylum and public assistance to gain permanent resident status and eventual citizenship.[22] In this case, race and politics go hand in hand, as the US determined there was little cause to grant political asylum to Haitians, whose repressive government the US supported. On the other hand, committed to toppling the Cuban government, the US has accepted almost every Cuban refugee and helped them establish an anti-Castro base in Miami. This is one of many outrages the US has perpetrated against the 'ripe fruit' ready to fall, as Secretary of State John Quincy Adams called Cuba in 1823, supporting President Monroe's famous 'doctrine' that claimed US hegemony over the New World.[23]

Even without its racial and sexual politics, the Danaids' flight in *Suppliant Women* finds parallels in the modern world, particularly in the current epidemic of dispossessed and fugitive peoples. Pelasgus accepts his city's responsibility to take in asylum seekers, an issue confronting governments today on an unprecedented scale. According to the UN High Commission on Refugees, the number of *official* refugees, internally displaced people, and asylum-seekers worldwide is just under 20 million people.[24] Many run into the anti-immigrant policies of recipient countries, policies that fail to address the underlying causes of the refugee problem: political instability, structural inequality, third-world debt, lack of human rights and the failure of global capitalism to provide for fair and adequate distribution of food and resources.

Although Greek tragedy has little to say directly on these matters, the plays overflow with refugees, exiles, suppliants, slaves and prisoners-of-war. Orestes arrives from (and returns to) exile in Aeschylus' *Choephori* and Euripides' *Electra*; Aegisthus knows from experience that 'exiles feed on empty hopes' in *Agamemnon* (1668); Oedipus and Polyneices in *Oedipus at Colonus*, Heracles at the end of *Heracles*, Medea in *Medea*, and Hippolytus in *Hippolytus* begin or end as exiles. Other fugitives, suppliants, or captives include Io in *Prometheus Bound*; Iolaus and Heracles' sons in *The Children of Heracles*; the Nurse and Chorus of Asian slaves in *Choephori*; Adrastus, the mothers of the Seven, and their grandsons in Euripides' *Suppliant Women*; Iole and the other female captives of Oechalia in *Women of Trachis*; the marooned Philoctetes in *Philoctetes*; Cassandra, the war-captive destined for slavery in *Agamemnon* and *Trojan Women*; Hecuba, Andromache, and the Trojan Women in *Trojan Women*, *Hecuba*, and *Andromache*; Iphigenia in *Iphigenia among the Taurians*; the Messenger from Thebes (an escaped prisoner-of-war) in Euripides' *Suppliant Women*; and even the shipwrecked satyrs of *Cyclops*. Various other foreign or enslaved personages appear as tutors, nurses, servants, and non-native Choruses in Greek tragedy. No comparable body of drama includes so many displaced or dispossessed people.

The fear that drives these characters from home, the terror of those conquered in war, and the desperation of those cut off from their past speak across time and culture. At the end of Euripides' *Electra*, for example, brother and sister understand what separation from each other and from their homeland really means:

Orestes: Oh my sister, after years finally to see you
and then in the same moment to be robbed of your love –
so I must leave you, you who are leaving me.
...
Electra: What other, greater grief is there
than to leave the borders of your native land?

Euripides *Electra* 1308-10, 1314-15

Characters who only witness the uprootedness of others suffer along with them. The Greek herald Talthybius in Euripides' *Trojan Women* describes Neoptolemus' departure with his war-prize Andromache (1126-46), whose farewell to her dead husband, child, and country 'drew many a tear from my own eyes' (1130-1). In Sophocles' *Women of Trachis*, Deianeira responds with 'terrible pity' (*oiktos deinos* 298) on seeing the women her husband has captured and enslaved, a sympathetic reaction that will be discussed further in Chapter 4.

Aeschylus gives us an extraordinary sense of what fear *feels like*,[25] but also of what it is good for. Aeschylus fought at Marathon, the quintessential hoplite battle, where the Greeks defeated the invading Persian army of king Darius. He also participated ten years later in the naval battle of Salamis, the unexpected Athenian victory that followed the Persian sack of Athens in 480 BCE (discussed in the Introduction). These remarkable triumphs support the view that Aeschylus' plays reflect the optimism of the early Athenian democracy. But we also sense the playwright's deep respect for fear in its various manifestations and transmutations. Unlike the Stoic idea of banishing fears, or the contemporary mantra of 'embracing' them,[26] Aeschylean tragedy confronts the fears that motivate human behaviour and explores the crucial role they play in forging a better society.

We see this clearly in the *Oresteia*, where fear is ubiquitous. It dwells in the house of Atreus (*Agamemnon* 1306, 1434), lurks in the shadows (154-5), pours down its fury like a rain of blood (1533-4). Fear infects the hearts of everyone it touches: Agamemnon (924, 933); Cassandra (1316); the Argive citizens (975-83); the household slaves (*Choephori* 46, 102, 167); Clytemnestra (*Cho.* 547); Orestes (286-90, 1024-5, 1052, *Eumenides* 88); the Pythia (*Eum.* 37-8). Fear keeps sleep at bay (Watchman, *Ag.* 14-15), or disrupts it with nightmarish visions (Clytemnestra, *Cho.* 32-5, 523-5). Fear dominates the past (the gagging of Iphigenia at *Agamemnon* 235-8, the feast of Thyestes at 1242-3), and it overshadows the future (Cassandra's prophecies, 1133-5).[27] At bottom, fear simply is in the world (*Cho.* 57-8, 585-6), and it takes the stage in the form of the Furies of the last play, spirits of vengeance who terrorize those they pursue.

Although defeated at the trial of Orestes (barely, as the votes are equal), the Furies hold the key to the prosperity of Athens. In a remarkable speech, Athena establishes *phobos* as the cornerstone of the new legal system she introduces to her city. She adopts the Furies' view (*Eum.* 517-30) on the essential role that fear plays in guaranteeing justice:

> On this site [the Areopagus] reverence
> and innate fear [*phobos*] will keep my citizens
> from injustice, day and night ...
> ...
> I advise my citizens: do not reverence or defend
> either lawlessness or despotism,
> and do not banish the terrible [*to deinon*] from your city.
> For no mortal can be just who has no fear [*dedoikôs mêden*].
>
> Aeschylus Eumenides 690-2, 696-9[28]

The incorporation of fear into the life of the city depends on the Furies' accepting Athena's offer to dwell permanently on Athenian soil. Far from banishing terror, Athens gives it a home, a transformation that Aeschylus marks theatrically with the final procession of the Furies out of the orchestra at the close of the trilogy. The newly enshrined deities make their way toward their new residence in a cave near the Areopagus, not far from the theatre of Dionysus.

Moving from the inauguration of civic institutions to the foundation of domestic life, tragedy returns time and again to children and the anxious fears they arouse. Tragic characters worry about the dangers of childbirth, the pitfalls of early development and education, the vulnerability of their offspring to illness and early death, the threat of youthful rebellion and rejection of parental authority. In her litany of the hardships facing women, Medea arrives at a memorable conclusion:

2. Tragedy and Fear

Men say that we live our lives free from danger,
safe at home, while they wage war with the spear.
They have it wrong. I would three times rather
hold a shield in battle than bear a single child.

Euripides Medea 248-51

Medea's judgement reflects the fact that childbirth in the ancient world posed tremendous risks for mother and child.[29] Although maternal and infant mortality rates in the modern period have dropped dramatically with improvements in public health and the control of infection, statistically childbirth remains a deadly threat to mothers, with over half a million women worldwide dying each year from pregnancy or childbirth.[30]

Assuming mother and newborn survive, parents in tragedy express great fear about what lies ahead. The Corinthian women in *Medea* offer the bleak view that humans are better off without these anxieties:

I think that those who remain
totally inexperienced in bearing children
have the advantage in happiness
over those who have them.
The childless never know
whether children bring joy or grief
and so they avoid all sorts of pain.
But those who have the sweet
joy of young ones in the house, I see
their whole lives worn away with care:
first, how to raise the children well
and provide for them, now and tomorrow;
next, whether all the pains taken
are worth it, or simply a waste of time.
Finally, the last misfortune of all
for those who are born mortal:
suppose you find enough to provide for your children,
and they reach the moment when they blossom
into adults, their character good and noble...
still a change of fortune can come by surprise,

and Death bear their bodies down to Hades.
How do we mortals benefit, when the gods –
on top of everything else –
burden us with the grievous woe
that goes by the name of children?

Euripides *Medea* 1090-1115

The strongest fear centres around the possibility that children will die young, leaving parents bereft and nullifying their labours on their children's behalf. As Medea contemplates murdering her sons rather than abandoning them to Jason and his new bride, she proclaims: 'In vain have I raised and nurtured you, my children,/ in vain did I go into labour, racked with pain/ in the throes of childbirth' (1029-31). When the Greeks seize her son Astyanax in *Trojan Women*, Andromache utters the same words: 'In vain did I go into labour' (Eur. *Tr.* 760). She describes her infant son's 'sweet breath of skin' (758), much like Medea: 'Oh your sweet touch!/ Oh the soft skin and fragrant breath of my children' (*Med.* 1074-5). Even Jason has similar reactions, when the full impact of his loss hits home: 'Oh god, how I long for the lovely smiles/ of my young boys, to hold them again in my arms./ .../ I beg you, let me touch again/ the soft skin of my children' (*Med.* 1399-1403). These wrenching evocations of dead offspring help us understand the Corinthian Women's earlier rejection of 'the grievous woe that goes by the name of children'.

In Euripides' *Suppliant Women*, Iphis comes to bring his son's corpse home for burial and to stop his daughter Evadne from harming herself. Crazed with grief for her dead husband, Evadne rejects her father's pleas and leaps to her death in Capaneus' funeral pyre. Iphis' response plumbs the desolation of parents who outlive their offspring:

I saw others having children, and longed for them too.
That longing has destroyed me.
If I had known what I now know, experiencing
what it means for a father to lose his children,
I would never have come to this misery.
...
She's gone. She used to put her lips
on my cheek, take my head

in her hands. Nothing sweeter
for an old father than his daughter. Boys
have strong spirits, but girls endear.
Lead me home, fast, faster,
back to the shadows, my old body
wasting away till I wither and die.

Euripides Suppliant Women
1087-91, 1099-1106[31]

Just as the future looks ominous to tragic characters, so too the memories of the past emphasize what is now absent and lost forever. The resulting emotions, strengthened by tragedy's disdain for the sentimental, make for an affective experience missing from much contemporary drama.

As noted in *Prometheus Bound* and *Oedipus Tyrannus*, children can instil fear by posing a threat to the powerful or by acting as agents of malignant fate. Stories of children destined to destroy themselves, their families, or their communities make up a good part of the tragic corpus. We find this motif particularly prominent in plays dealing with infamous royal houses: the house of Labdacus in Thebes (Laius, Oedipus, Eteocles, Polyneices, Antigone) and in Argos (via Polyneices, who leads the Argives against Thebes); the house of Tantalus (which includes Atreus, Thyestes, Agamemnon, Aegisthus, Iphigenia, Orestes, Electra) in Mycenae or Argos; the line of Acrisius, grandson of Hypermestra and Lynkeus (mentioned above in Aeschylus' *Danaid* trilogy), fated to die at the hands of his daughter's (Danae's) son, the subject of several lost plays of Aeschylus (*Polydectes*, *Children of Phorcys*, the satyr-play *Netdrawers*), Sophocles (*Acrisius, Danae, Men of Larissa*), and Euripides (*Danae, Dictys*); the house of Priam at Troy, where Hecuba dreams that she gave birth to a flaming torch (Paris) that will cause Troy's fall, the subject of lost plays by Sophocles and Euripides (both entitled *Alexandros*, another name for Paris); Aleos of Tegea, who receives an oracle that, if his daughter Auge has a son, he will kill Aleos' own sons, the background to lost plays by Sophocles (*Sons of Aleus, Eurypylus, Mysoi*), Euripides (*Telephus, Auge*), and Aeschylus (*Telephus*); and even Odysseus, fated to die at the hands of Telegonus, his son by Circe, the subject of Sophocles' lost *Odysseus Acanthoplex*.[32]

In these tragedies, doom moves across generations, linking parents to their children and ancestors to their descendants. Antigone carries the seed of self-destruction inherited from her father (and half-brother) Oedipus and her mother Jocasta; Oedipus' sons Eteocles and Polyneices, cursed by their father, bring war on Thebes and Argos, and death to each other. Some scholars think that the dramatization of such royal disasters exposes the threat posed by aristocratic families, reflecting democratic fears that elites might lead Athens astray or undermine its radical form of government.[33] For all the tension between 'royalty' and the democratic *polis*, however, the plays seem to focus on the tragedy implicit in *all* human generations, reminding us that the past is never past. It lives on in human beings as a necessary condition of their birth, and it affects their future (and the future of their offspring) in ways that cannot be controlled.

The world that tragic characters inhabit reflects the world that prior generations have helped to make. To generalize boldly, many of us today (particularly in the United States) have a love-affair with the 'now', as if the past didn't matter and the future was there for the taking, waiting to be mastered. One sees this phenomenon most blindingly in the extraordinary discourse around 'mutually assured destruction' (MAD), a popular policy subject during the 'Cold War', and more recently in the cavalier decisions regarding nuclear waste. By the year 2010, the United States inventory of spent nuclear fuel will reach 62,000 metric tons, which the government proposes to store permanently in an earthquake-active region of Nevada – Yucca Mountain – where it will remain radioactive for more than 10,000 years (and dangerously so for over 1,000 years, which is almost five times longer than the United States has existed as a nation).[34] Because the capacity of Yucca Mountain is 70,000 metric tons (63,000 metric tons of commercial spent fuel, 2,333 metric tons of defence spent nuclear fuel, and 4,667 metric tons of defence high-level radioactive waste), the US will need to find *another* storage area in the near future for the additional radioactive material currently being produced.

Countering our arrogant myth of an uncontaminated future, Greek tragedy emphasizes continuities over time. For the Greeks, a present and future cut off from the past signalled, at best, a dangerous illusion. The protracted nature of human experience (both spatially and temporally) might prove disastrous or it might offer salvation, but it cannot be denied. In *Prometheus Bound*, for instance, Zeus fears he will father a son who will topple him from power, just as Zeus overthrew his own father Cronos, and Cronos vanquished his father Ouranos. For Zeus, the future looms as a cyclical pattern from which he hopes to escape. Prometheus, on the other hand, looks to the cycle of human procreation for the source of his salvation, in particular to the thirteenth generation descended from the original offspring of Io and Zeus, namely Heracles, who eventually will liberate Prometheus from his rock-bound torment. Although bitter enemies, both Prometheus and Zeus are inextricably bound to a future engendered by the past.

Playwrights of the modern and contemporary period have taken up the themes of transgenerational inheritance and cyclical disaster with a vengeance. From Ibsen (*Ghosts, Rosmersholm, Hedda Gabler*) to O'Neill (*Mourning Becomes Electra, Long Day's Journey into Night*), Miller (*All My Sons, Death of a Salesman*) to Shepard (*Curse of the Starving Class, Buried Child, True West*), the sins, crimes, and obsessions of parents break out again in their offspring, usually with destructive consequences. What has changed from the time of Greek tragedy involves the reasons *why* such repetition occurs. In Ibsen's *Ghosts*, inherited venereal disease works its physiological destruction; in *Rosmersholm*, the childhood trauma of sexual abuse (incest) dooms the future; in *Hedda Gabler*, a dominating (absent) father casts a suicidal shadow over his daughter's life.[35]

Known for his sagas of dysfunctional American families, Sam Shepard emphasizes how a shared temperament can infect a household, explained by Emma in *Curse of the Starving Class*:

> A short fuse they call it. Runs in the family. His father was just like him. And his father before him. Wesley [Emma's brother] is just like Pop, too. Like liquid dynamite .... It's chemical. The same thing that makes him drink. Something in the blood. Hereditary. Highly explosive .... Nitroglycerine. That's what it's called. Nitroglycerine .... In the blood.[36]

Miller also deals with hereditary influences, but he tends to focus on broader cultural factors reflecting post-war American culture, including materialism, consumerism, self-aggrandizement, and petty greed, which lead to familial crises and social breakdown (*All My Sons, Death of a Salesman*).

In his 'working notes' on *Mourning Becomes Electra*, an adaptation that conflates Aeschylus' *Oresteia* and Sophocles' *Electra*, Eugene O'Neill asks the following question: 'Is it possible to get [a] modern psychological approximation of [the] Greek sense of fate into such a play, which an intelligent audience of today, possessed by no belief in gods or supernatural retribution, could accept and be moved by?' A few years later, he returns to the same issue: 'Greek tragedy plot idea – No matter in what period ... [it] is laid, must remain a modern psychological drama.'[37] For O'Neill, the unconscious – as the source of uncontrollable drives and heroic resistance – offers a modern equivalent of fate.

In many of O'Neill's plays, characters attempt to exorcise their psychological devils by a kind of theatrical Freudian therapy. According to psychoanalytic theory, bringing latent or repressed fears to consciousness allows patients to align better their interior and exterior realities. Freud understood this process as a quest for rational explanations of apparently irrational or aberrant behaviour. Although lacking scientific confirmation by controlled experiment, Freud's views on psychic turmoil have had a remarkable impact on the theatre, especially in individualist plays interested in exposing and exploiting private demons. Freudian theory has joined genetics, sociology, anthropology, and legal theory to establish the horizon of much modern bourgeois drama, where the formation, deformation, and revelation of 'character' loom large, and dramatic plots focus on psychological struggle, individual success or failure, and personal fulfilment.

To risk a crass generalization, fear in modern drama tends toward the private and inner, the kind of angst that carries little political significance or public impact. The issues that terrify remain personal, not social, reflecting the pervasive influence of television drama, Hollywood heroics, and the narcissism of home video and the camcorder. The drama of the troubled psyche settles comfortably indoors, finding its appropriate setting in the living room, dining room or bedroom (discussed in Chapter 1). Alternatively, experimental or avant-garde productions feature the fantasies of the artist-auteur, whose highly personal imagery replaces narratives grounded in the shared material of the public world. Contemporary theatre prefers the personal, the odd, and the idiosyncratic rather than the social and political, reflecting the individualistic direction of capitalist society and the profitable disinclination among artists to engage public issues from an unpleasant or disturbing perspective.

Although removed in form and spirit from Greek tragedy, the political theatre of Georg Büchner, Nikolai Gogol, George Bernard Shaw, (early) Gerhart Hauptmann, Maxim Gorky, Georg Kaiser, Sean O'Casey, Ernst Toller, Erwin Piscator, Bertolt Brecht, Max Frisch, The Group Theatre, The Federal Theatre Project, The Theatre Workshop (Joan Littlewood, Brendan Behan, etc.), Peter Weiss, Friedrich Dürrenmatt, John Osborne, John Arden, Margaretta D'Arcy, Edward Bond, Caryl Churchill, Brian Friel, Howard Barker, Howard Brenton, Tony Harrison, Tony Kushner, Naomi Wallace, and other kindred spirits remains rooted in historical, social, and economic circumstance. These political artists acknowledge the world as made, with cultural and material forces dictating patterns of thought and behaviour. Like Greek tragedy, their work does not shrink the world down to the consciousness of the unique individual, autonomous and free to suffer, change, grow, fall, or triumph within a maelstrom of private angst.

To bring these generalities home, let us examine the fears that emerge in Irish playwright Marina Carr's recent adaptation of Euripides' *Medea*, entitled *By the Bog of Cats*.[38] In Carr's play, the traveller Hester Swane has been 'put aside' by an aspiring Carthage Kilbride (the Jason figure) who marries into a respectable landowning family. Fearful of her future, Hester is also haunted by her past, particularly the murder of her brother, whose body she had disposed of secretly with Carthage's help.[39] On Carthage's wedding night, Hester burns the farmhouse and livestock of his new family, and prepares to kill herself. In the play's climactic scene, however, she realizes that her suicide will leave her daughter Josie abandoned, just as Hester was abandoned as a young girl by her own mother. Inflamed by the thought, Hester kills her daughter before killing herself.

Deeper than her fears of rejection, of living without the man she loves, of having to leave her community, Hester is terrified that her daughter will live the same despondent life that she has known, always waiting in vain for her mother's return across the Bog of Cats. Beautifully written, intelligently adapted, and deeply rooted in Ireland and Irish folk memory, Carr's play nonetheless relies on a specific childhood trauma to produce the fear that motivates Hester to take the innocent life of her child.

In Euripides' *Medea*, on the other hand, various fears and anxieties operate over the course of the play, but none more powerfully than Medea's fear of being laughed at by her enemies. On six occasions she explicitly refers to this fear, each time using a form of the verb 'mock' or 'laugh at' (*gelaô*). The idea stems from the traditional Greek belief that one should hate (and harm) one's enemies and love (and help) one's friends, with the corollary that the public laughter of those who hate you (and whom you hate) represents intolerable humiliation. Debating whether to kill her children or take them with her to Athens, Medea asks the fatal question, 'Do I want to earn the laughter/ of my enemies by leaving them unpunished?' (1049-50). After the filicide, an abject Jason reminds her that 'you too suffer and share the grief I feel', to which Medea responds, 'Yes, but my pain is worth it if you cannot laugh at me' (1361-2).

The reasons for Medea's actions reflect a central moral tenet of Athenian society, one deeply embedded in male-dominated ideology linked to 'face saving', competition, warfare, and a highly polarized notion of friend and enemy.[40] Although non-male and non-Greek, Euripides' Medea has assimilated the values of her new culture all too well. Far from the barbarian that Jason calls her at the end of the play, Medea adheres so faithfully to the Greek idea of harming enemies to avoid their mockery that she slays her own children rather than the guilty Jason, something she considers doing earlier in the play (at lines 271 and 375). The Nurse's hope that Medea might 'work against enemies and not friends' (95) turns on itself, for she kills those she loves to make her enemy suffer.

Medea's fear of her enemy's laughter reflects a widespread social and cultural practice, whose destructive consequences the play demonstrates with great force, a subject to which we will return in Chapter 4, 'Tragedy and Ideology'. For the Greek audience, the desire to punish one's enemies and the fear of enduring their laughter was real enough, engrained in public consciousness. It did not represent the psychic results of some personal trauma, as in the case of Carr's Hester Swane, who suffers from an absent mother. By focusing on Medea's fear of mockery, Euripides exposes the dangers inherent in the principle that guides her actions, extending the compass of the play from a wronged woman to a skewed system of cultural values.

But this exposé of dangerous moral principles also reflects the play's historical moment. *Medea* was first performed in 431 BCE, shortly before the Peloponnesian War formally broke out between Athens and Sparta, the disastrous internecine conflict that dominated the Greek world in the last third of the fifth century. Hostilities between Athens and Corinth, an ally of Sparta, already had begun in 433 BCE on Kerkyra (Corfu), and the Corinthian setting of *Medea* may allude to that engagement. Moreover, the fact that the play ends with Medea heading for the very city where the audience sat in the theatre of Dionysus may have suggested the violence of war that was on its way to Athens.

When the Chorus first learn of Medea's plan to kill her children, they sing an ode praising Athens as a city graced by prosperity, natural beauty, and the arts (824-45). However, the tone of the ode shifts radically when the Chorus ask how that same city could welcome the bloodstained killer of her own children (846-65). Symbolizing the outbreak of war, Medea receives special scrutiny as a future Athenian, and so does the fear that motivates her filicide. Euripides' tragedy resonates far beyond the protagonist's individual situation, suggesting a deep fissure in the moral and political values of her new city. As war enters Athens, *Medea* reveals the insanity implicit in the popular doctrine that fear of an enemy's laughter constitutes a valid reason for bloodshed. To harm one's enemies by killing one's own is self-destructive; war between the Greek states takes the principle to its logical extreme.

We have seen the prominent role that the emotion of fear plays in Greek tragedy, from facing the panic of battle to confronting the uncertainties of life, from conquering fear through sympathy and solidarity to examining the deadly effects of a creed based on dreading an enemy's laughter. As an explanation of human behaviour, fear in Greek tragedy trades on the public and cultural far more than the private and personal. The idea that dramatic causalities are hermetically sealed within an individual psyche plays no part in the radical theatre of the Greeks, as we will discuss in the next chapter, 'The Fate of Agency, the Agency of Fate'.

3

The Fate of Agency,
the Agency of Fate

There is no evil greater for humans
than fate imposed by necessity.

Sophocles *Ajax* 485-6

Be original, an individual
Like Dr. Pepper

Television soft-drink
commercial, 2002

'The tragic problem', Vernant suggested some 30 years ago, is epitomized in Orestes' outcry at the point of murdering his mother: *ti
drasô*; 'What shall I do?'[1] The question reflects a confluence of forces
that find their object and outlet in Orestes: traditional expectations
of revenge, the requirements of patrimony, a son's duty to his father,
a family member's obligation to his *oikos* ('household', an irreducible
aspect of identity in Greek society), a prince's responsibility to his
kingdom, and the pressures of divine sanction and command.[2] Orestes himself describes the occasions that inform against him:

> He [Apollo] told of wrath that springs from the earth,
> and the forms of plague it takes against men:
> a leprous ulcer that grows on the skin,
> sinking its fangs, spreading a white down
> that devours the flesh to the core.
> And he spoke of other assaults of the Furies,
> born and bred from my father's blood:
> eyes in the dark, staring;
> a shaft of light from the dead,

demanding vengeance for fallen kin;
nightmare and madness, my mind troubled
like a storm at sea, driven from the city,
my flesh beaten and cut by their goad of bronze.
Aeschylus *Choephori* 278-90[3]

Orestes' litany demonstrates the 'overdetermination' of Greek tragic characters, the fact that both human and divine forces conjoin in motivating their actions.[4] As a result, some classicists claim – wrongly, in my view – that the ancient Greeks (and their representatives on stage) did not act 'for themselves' in a way that we could credit with psychological depth or (free) agency. Clearly, Orestes feels both internal and external compulsions to matricide, and in facing those compulsions he – in a meaningful sense – meets his fate. No one but Orestes must commit this crime, which is another way of saying that murdering his mother Clytemnestra and her lover Aegisthus for killing his father Agamemnon is part and parcel of what it means to *be* Orestes. Who he is is not simply up to him to choose, but having been chosen 'Orestes', Orestes' choices begin.

At the moment of crisis this overdetermined and fate-driven character cries out, 'Pylades, what should I do? Fear to kill my mother?' The question is not rhetorical, as Aeschylus makes dramatically clear when the otherwise silent Pylades answers:

> *Pylades*: What then becomes of the oracles of Apollo
> delivered at Delphi, and the oaths you swore?
> Count all men your enemy, but not the gods.
> *Orestes*: I judge you the victor; you advise me well.
Aeschylus *Choephori* 899-903

Outside of a god appearing on high, Aeschylus could not establish more clearly the Olympian force behind the matricide.[5] Orestes' dilemma generates a god-like response from Pylades, making the impending murder both chosen and constrained, and therefore fully tragic.

In *Agamemnon*, Orestes' father faces a similar dilemma, dramatized by the Chorus in the *parodos*. At Aulis the prophet Calchas declares that Agamemnon must sacrifice his daughter Iphigenia to

66

assuage the anger of the goddess Artemis. Only by this perverse deed can the Greek fleet sail for Troy. The Chorus evoke the many forces weighing on Agamemnon's decision: his role as commander-in-chief, the contrary winds that keep the Greeks from embarking, the boredom and war-eagerness of the soldiers, the clarity of Calchas' prophecy, the evidence of Artemis' anger, and the fact that the victim is Agamemnon's own daughter, 'the treasure of my house', as he calls her (*Ag.* 208). In a phrase that captures the tragic combination of choice and necessity, Agamemnon 'put on the harness-strap of necessity' (*Ag.* 218). That is, Agamemnon actively chose to do ('He put on') what he had no choice in or control over ('the harness-strap of necessity').[6] Orestes' decision in *Choephori* represents a similar paradox of free choice and coercion, but one that Aeschylus dramatizes fully. Orestes asks his tragic question and makes his decision in plain view of the victim, the Chorus, and the audience.

In the *Oresteia*, the effects of human agency (just like its 'causes') extend beyond the actors and their local context. They stretch out to include the gods – Zeus, Artemis, Hermes, Apollo, Athena, the Furies (the last three dominate *Eumenides*) – and the city where the performance originally took place. The foundation of the original Athenian homicide court and the incorporation of the Furies into Athens effectively replace the Argive house of Atreus as the focus of the drama. But the trilogy's movement (forward in time, closer in space) depends on an intricate set of relationships involving kinship, politics, religion, myth, and a complex weave of poetic imagery. In this world, action at one point on the dramatic web reverberates over its entire surface.[7] Choices by Atreus and Thyestes, by Paris and Helen, by Agamemnon, by the Greek army, by Clytemnestra, by Aegisthus, by Orestes and Electra, by the Chorus of household slaves, by the Nurse, by the jury of Athenians have far-ranging consequences that none of the agents fully anticipates.

In another culture, we might expect such a tragic vision to produce a sense of powerlessness before the multiple forces that lie beyond human control. But not in fifth-century Athens. 'Fate' may influence human choices, but the fact that their end-point and goal (what the Greeks call *telos*) lies in the city of the audience indicates the crucial importance of grappling with past decisions now. The expansive terrain of the *Oresteia* shows the multiple effects of those choices, culminating in the foundation of the court on the Areopagus. The basis of democratic justice, manifest in the trial of Orestes, lies in the belief that individual judgements – when delivered collectively – can serve the social order. This idea is rooted in the power and purpose of human agency, given dramatic form in Aeschylus' trilogy.

An interesting example of individual and collective choice occurs in the debate among the twelve Chorus members after hearing Agamemnon's offstage death-cries (*Ag.* 1346-71). Half the Chorus 'vote' for action, the other half favour caution. Their slightly comic deliberation foreshadows the Athenian jury's split decision over Orestes' guilt in *Eumenides*. Here, as in other proleptic scenes, the trilogy gathers the past towards the future, developing a kind of virtual (but hardly idealized) history of how things came to be, built on decisions in the past. In recovering the radical nature of Greek tragedy, a central challenge lies in making such human deliberation and choice a matter of moment today.[8]

To explore in detail the workings of agency and fate – and the related concepts of choice, intentionality, causality, consciousness, self, and 'the subject' – lies beyond the scope of this book. However, we can point out some essential continuities that link our understanding to that of fifth-century Athens. In the past, many scholars denied that the ancient Greeks had (or could comprehend) such concepts as the will, the autonomous self, and the possibility of moral agency. However, the work of several scholars – Albin Lesky, Alvin Gouldner, Patricia Easterling, Christopher Pelling, Bernard Williams, Douglas Cairns, Martha Nussbaum – has helped us understand that 'seeing the self as other, and the other as a kind of self' was not a concept foreign to fifth-century Athenians. Nor were the concomitant notions of agency, choice, and responsibility.[9] These concepts involve an internalized sense of right behaviour – based on the assumption that 'a rational agent must choose reasons that would appeal to other rational agents similarly circumstanced' – and the self-conscious awareness that individual decisions affect one's own life within (and without) the workings of fate. As Gouldner puts it, 'The development of Greek drama premises self-conscious individuals who can do what Agamemnon asks in *Hecuba*: "Put yourself in my position".'[10]

It remains a common assumption, for example, that Sophocles'

3. The Fate of Agency, the Agency of Fate

Oedipus Tyrannus is a play that denies human freedom and the efficacy of individual choice. In his classic refutation of this view, Dodds observes that 'certain of Oedipus' past actions were fate-bound, but everything that he does on the stage from first to last he does as a free agent'.[11] Nonetheless, the idea that Greek tragic figures are pawns in a cosmic game, or puppets in the hands of fate, persists in the popular imagination. For this reason, many consider tragedy either too cruel and inhuman to warrant interest, or too out-of-touch with contemporary reality to justify unadapted performance. Old taboos have lost their sting, and the insights of psychology and the demands of individualism render the very idea of tragedy anachronistic.

Such views reflect and sustain the popular Western model of progress, understood as the movement from primitive ignorance to modern insight. This model assumes that progress consists in the following:

- A change from political, religious, and collective control over behaviour (a 'shame culture') to an internally conceived notion of autonomy, personal freedom, and individual truth (a 'guilt culture').[12]
- The advance from a blinkered literalism based on actions to a nuanced psychological appreciation of personal feelings, intentions, and desires.
- The growth out of superstition and myth (the world as 'fate') into scientific and technical understanding (the world as a place we master and fashion).

As the *Oresteia* and *Oedipus Tyrannus* demonstrate, Greek tragedy concerns itself with progress, but not as an endless expansion of human capacity, power, and domination. What progress there is emerges through the experience of the tragic, *not* through its avoidance or transcendence. The Chorus of *Agamemnon* put the case plainly:

> Zeus sets men on the path of wisdom,
> establishing the rule:
> we learn by suffering.

Drip by drip, in place of sleep
the memory of pain on the heart;
against our will comes wisdom,
the grace of gods by force ...
Aeschylus *Agamemnon* 176-82[13]

Operating on human beings from within *and* without, fate sets harsh limits on human desires and accomplishments, as Oedipus, Orestes, and other tragic heroes force us to see.

The Greeks had several words for what we call 'fate', chief among them *moira* ('portion', 'lot') and *tuchê* ('what happens', 'what befalls', 'what comes one's way').[14] We might understand *moira* as the circumstances into which we are born. These circumstances include our biological inheritance and endowment; the realities of lengthy childhood dependency; the nature of language acquisition and physical development; the powerful influences of family, culture, and society; and the physical processes of growth, illness, decay and death. Although the word can mean different things in Hesiod than it does in Plato, *moira* can always refer to 'death',[15] precisely the meaning that invests human choice with significance. In a world without death, decisions become inconsequential because they remain eternally open to change – the 'fate' of the Homeric gods, who never die. For this reason, the Olympians constitute 'spheres of power but not of significance', in Redfield's memorable phrase.[16]

If *moira* represents both the specifics that define each individual and the general end that mortality imposes on all of us, then *tuchê* indicates the unexpected or unpredictable events that lie along the way, what we call 'chance', 'luck', 'fortune', whatever 'happens' to us. Although *moira* appears to be prior to *tuchê*, its importance – as in biological inheritance, for example – lies in what has yet to come. The past may be 'the tragic tense' because it is beyond recall,[17] but *moira* in Greek tragedy matters only when it emerges in the present. In other words, Oedipus' patricide and incest do not constitute tragic actions until he (and Jocasta before him) recognize them as such.

To adopt the current biological model, *moira* resembles DNA, a set of predetermined proclivities whose actualization emerges only with the passage of time. *Tuchê* is what comes along during that passage, which of course hinges on what has gone before, like a train wreck that may or may not involve us, depending on whether we caught that train or missed it. In the case of Oedipus, his *moira* involves being the son of Laius and Jocasta of the royal house of Thebes; his *tuchê* includes (among other things) coming upon the unrecognized Laius at a place where three roads meet.

We humans have little if any influence over *moira*, whereas the decisions we make can affect our *tuchê*, what we 'run into'. On Agamemnon's return home, the Chorus address him as 'King who ravaged Troy,/ offspring of Atreus ...' (*Ag.* 783-4). Their greeting embraces the interlocking causes that will lead to Agamemnon's death, 'that which he incurred voluntarily and that to which he has fallen heir'.[18] Agamemnon has no choice in the identity of his father Atreus, but he does play a decisive role in the war at Troy and at the city's fall. Both the inherited curse on his line (involving Atreus' butchery of Thyestes' children) and his own actions vis-à-vis Troy (Iphigenia's sacrifice, the Greek sacrilege at the sack of the city) affect what 'happens' to Agamemnon when he comes home.

I daresay the modern imagination implicitly accepts some version of *tuchê*, recognizing that no one can anticipate everything that comes down the road. Nonetheless, so-called 'advanced' societies display a voracious appetite for control (or the illusion of control) over their internal and external worlds. We see this in the boom in suburban gated communities, designed to protect property and keep unwelcome elements outside the defensive perimeter. The extraordinary rise in prison construction and incarceration reflects the same attitude. On a larger geopolitical scale, the United States government remains committed to a 'missile defence shield' in spite of the system's outlandish cost, technical impracticality, tactical ineffi-ciency, and ultimate danger.[19]

Turning our attention to the natural world, we hear that genetic engineering, particularly in agriculture, promises an internal 'de-fence shield' against natural processes like decay and rot. In many cases, plant genes are modified to make them resistant to pesticides and herbicides produced by the same company that bio-engineers the food crops. This 'protects' the plant from otherwise harmful chemi-cals, even as it guarantees farmers' dependency on those same chemicals to maximize their yield. For example, 'Roundup Ready' genetically modified corn and soybeans from Monsanto cannot be harmed by the application of Monsanto's Round-Up weed killer, meaning that the two products operate in tandem. One can apply the herbicide without worrying about killing the corn or beans, which are now genetically immune to Round-Up. Under the guise of increasing our control over food production, multinational agribusinesses continue their profit-driven 'progress' more or less unchecked.[20]

On an individual level, consumers choose from a smorgasbord of security and alarm systems, personal safety and self-defence devices, health tonics and food supplements, dietary regimens, exercise equipment, and drugs to ward off everything from bad breath to heart attacks. Cell phones, wireless internet access, portable entertainment units, and hand-held global positioning systems (GPSs) ensure that we never drop out of contact, never get lost, never find ourselves on our own. Moving from satellites high above to cells deep within, research on DNA and the human genome promises extraordinary advances in disease prevention, while preparing the market for 'designer babies' – genetically secure from brown eyes, short stature, male-pattern balding, the 'wrong' sexual preference, and a range of other 'developmental disorders'.[21]

We live in a world – as the second epigraph to this chapter suggests – where originality is only a sip away, and anyone (except, perhaps, the one billion humans who survive on less than $1 per day) can buy it for herself. Special soaps fight pollution; an improved formula defeats cavities; the right pill wards off insomnia; the macho cigarette delivers manliness; the latest scent makes you irresistible; the fastest car buys freedom; designer clothes get the girl, or the guy, or both. Fitting seamlessly into consumer ideology, national 'defence' is merely an extension of the individual's right to purchase power, well-being, and security. New products are developed and deployed, from daisy-cutters and cluster bombs to the B-1 bomber. Asserting mastery over the globe, the US reinforces the myth that these strategies make America, its citizens, and its 'friends' safe. Like Sophocles' Oedipus, or the Greek states in Thucydides, we find ourselves promoting what we fear by our very efforts to avert it.[22]

But such self-endangering myths are no accident. The modern passion for control reflects and feeds into the consumerism basic to capitalist economies. The drive to buy and possess fosters interrelated and often contradictory myths about human nature, economic profit, 'free' markets, and democracy. One such myth claims that people are insatiably greedy and driven by self-interest; another assumes that individual uniqueness is proof of freedom, reflecting a combination of inner and outer 'properties' that are (paradoxically) available for purchase. We even are told that personal consumption represents a cooperative virtue, because consumerism plays an essential role in a healthy economy (and someone else can handle the garbage).

The corporate world feeds us the myth that maximizing private profit benefits society at large, because wealth trickles down to the dispossessed and disadvantaged. We learn that picking leaders in open elections, choosing goods in free markets, and selling our labour to the highest bidder are all manifestations of political freedom and democracy. We are encouraged to think of economic growth as a limitless concept, and to consider *everything* as something owned or for sale, from intellectual property to drinking water, from medical care to education. We take it on faith that sufficient personal effort can enable each and every individual in the system to 'win'. We believe that we can purchase protection from – and power over – our own inadequacies, just as with sufficient resources we can control the world before us. Finally, we know that this process never ends because the world keeps changing, producing new dangers and requiring innovative products to keep those new threats at bay.

A glance at the commercial theatre indicates how these myths infect artistic practice and foster the 'privatization' of public events. In the Broadway house where the Disney-produced musical *The Lion King* has been running for several years, exits at the end of the show funnel the audience into gift shops, where they can take home memories of their recent theatrical experience in tangible form. Should the audience resist at that point, fast-food chains (with Disney licensing contracts) and globally-run department stores offer *Lion King* videos, video-games, dolls, books, comics, figurines, drinking glasses, sketch-pads, lunch pails, thermoses, pencils, sweaters, T-shirts, head-bands, stuffed animals, trading cards – a list longer than the sexual conquests of Zeus. We can 'own' the experience of live theatre after the fact, and Disney shows us how.[23] And we needn't give a thought to the threatened habitat of real lions in the ever-shrinking savannah.

73

The illusion of mastery through the exercise of power and privilege seems a far cry from the Greek tragic sense that humans dwell in a world they have not created and cannot control. Time and again tragedy reveals the vulnerability of its characters and the limits of their knowledge and power. As we might suspect, death proves the point: it is universal, unavoidable, and invariably seems to come at the wrong time.[24] If Greek tragedy has an overarching ethical dimension, it consists in recognising these human limits and finding our proper relationship to them. Time and again the plays expose the fragility of what characters take to be certain and secure. Although such lessons appear simple and easy to grasp, the contemporary mythology sketched above makes them harder to learn than they might be. Greek tragedy has much to teach us on this score, and it offers its lessons with concision and power.

Unique among extant tragedies, Aeschylus' *Persians* dramatizes a contemporary fifth-century event, Athens' defeat of the Persian invaders in the naval battle at Salamis in 480 BCE. Unlike Oedipus' patricide in *Oedipus Tyrannus* or Agamemnon's assassination in *Agamemnon*, 'fate' in *Persians* (the defeat of Xerxes' expedition) finds its confirmation not in the mythic tradition but in historical fact. Most of those attending the City Dionysia in 472 experienced some aspect of the Persian invasion firsthand. Athens evacuated its civilian population in 480 and again in 479, anticipating the sack and burning of the city that occurred on both occasions. In an unexpected victory, the Athenians – with their metics (resident aliens) and slaves – defeated the Persian fleet at Salamis, and the subsequent land victory at Plataea led by the Spartans drove the foreigners from Greece.[25] As noted in Chapter 1, the destruction wreaked by the Persian invasion remained visible from the theatre of Dionysus when the play was first performed.

To merge these historical facts with the workings of fate and agency, Aeschylus introduces two numinous events: the dream of the Persian queen (mother of Xerxes), and the prophetic utterances of her dead husband Darius, who 'prophesies after the event'.[26] Atossa's nightmare and Darius' ghost convey information about the invasion of Greece that the original audience would have known from experience. By their inclusion, however, Aeschylus also places the Persian defeat within a broader ethical framework. Both the dream and the

74

prophecy associate Xerxes' territorial expansion – 'yoking' the Hellespont via a bridge of ships – with the moral outrage of *hubris*, the Greek word for insolence, contempt, and excessive violence.[27]

The classic example of individual *hubris* is Capaneus, one of the Argive 'seven against Thebes', who boasts that he will seize the city in spite of Zeus' warnings, a subject broached in Aeschylus' *Seven Against Thebes*, Sophocles' *Antigone* and *Oedipus at Colonus*, and Euripides' *Suppliant Women* and *Phoenician Women*. When Capaneus mounts a ladder against the walls of Thebes, Zeus blasts him with a lighting bolt, and the incinerated hero falls to his death, an object lesson to those whose ambition rises too high.[28] In *Persians*, Xerxes' invasion of Greece exemplifies *hubris* on an imperial scale. The Persian defeat offers a warning to other states with grand designs, perhaps even Athens, poised in 472 to establish its own empire, for which it later suffered the consequences.

In the modern world, the notion of limits – moral, political, economic, scientific – has come under increasing scrutiny. Who sets those limits, and who gives anyone the right to do so? How does one account for different boundaries on appropriate behaviour in different societies? Confronting such variations, how can one posit 'natural' limits imposed or guaranteed by the cosmos, a view that approximates the ancient Greek position? On the other hand, a growing number of people insist on the necessity for limits if we are to preserve the environment on which human life depends. Scientists who study the issue agree that the earth's atmosphere cannot survive the uncontrolled emission of greenhouse gases, the primary cause of global warming that threatens the vitality of the planet. Ice caps and glaciers are melting, rivers and ocean levels rising, and low-lying regions face inundation. Global climate patterns are changing, reducing the ameliorative affects of ocean movements like the Gulf Stream, which in turn may undermine traditional agricultural production and wreak havoc on various populations.

To be sure, the Greeks viewed nature and natural phenomena differently. Due to their low population and low-level technology, the ancient Greeks had much less impact on the environment than we do. Whatever effect they did have seemed of little immediate concern to them. Nonetheless, the notions of *hubris*, *moira*, and *tuchê* suggest an implicit recognition that unbounded expansion (in any direction) does violence to the cosmos, and the cosmos will take its revenge. An aspect of that revenge involves human agents working over time, as we see in the *Oresteia*. In *Persians* the agency of fate has a collective face, for it is the resistance of democratic Athens that raises an effective barrier to Xerxes' imperial designs. In Aeschylus' play, the Athenians' love of freedom, their hatred of tyranny, their loyalty to the land, their selflessness in its defence, and their daring military strategy align with Zeus' preservation of the 'moral order of the world', as Winnington-Ingram puts it.[29]

Only on rare occasions in tragedy do we witness a complete disjunction between human behaviour and divine purpose, as in the god-sent madness that strikes the innocent hero of Euripides' *Heracles*. Generally in tragedy, human characters wielding immoderate force contribute to their own demise: Xerxes in *Persians*; Agamemnon (and to a lesser extent Clytemnestra, Aegisthus, and Orestes) in the *Oresteia*; the sons of Aegyptos in *Suppliant Women*; Creon in *Antigone* (and offstage in Euripides' *Suppliant Women*); the seven against Thebes in Aeschylus' play (and in Euripides' *Suppliant Women* and *Phoenician Women*); Theseus in *Hippolytus*; the Greeks, Polymestor, and eventually Hecuba in *Hecuba*; Lycus in *Heracles*; Pentheus in *Bacchae*; and the Greek army in *Trojan Women*. All these dramatic agents engage in excessive acts that contribute to the disasters that befall them. The Greeks knew (at least in principle) that *hubris* is punished, that power corrupts, and that the powerful tend to forget how tenuous their mastery is until they bring destruction on themselves and others.

Like playwrights who followed them, Greek tragedians found the catastrophes of the great of more dramatic interest than the suffering of the weak, for the simple reason that they seem potentially avoidable. By definition, those with power can affect the world in which they live. Sadly, this fact slips easily from view, as indicated by a *New York Times* story headlined 'Two Worlds Paired by War: Life or Death, as Luck Will Have It' (31 December 2001). We learn that the situation of Afghan peasants during the 'Allied' bombing campaign was no different from that of New Yorkers at the World Trade Center or US military personnel at the Pentagon on 11 September 2001: 'Chance was the ultimate arbiter, and good luck and bad were best expressed by the locations of one's feet when the planes came in, when the buildings came down, or when bombs landed on a house.'[30] The article makes no distinction between impoverished Afghans and well-off Americans; it ignores the gross disparity in power and opportunity that separates the two sets of victims, both before and after the horrors from the sky; it fails to differentiate the terrorism of a clandestine group using box-cutters and commercial aircraft from the state-sponsored terror of the greatest military power on earth, one that wields enormous influence over media outlets like the *New York Times*. Chance may be the ultimate arbiter, and death will find us all, but the *tuchê* that leads cluster-bombs to fall on a Red Cross warehouse, a 'Taliban village', and a mud-brick mosque is not the same *tuchê* that leads to a suicide mission at the Pentagon and World Trade Center. Unlike the *New York Times* article, Greek tragedy shows *tuchê* affecting the powerful, who help bring disaster *on themselves*. By showing past choices affecting present disaster, tragedy demonstrates how *hubris* paradoxically serves the inexorable ends of *moira*.

Returning to *Persians*, we should note that Aeschylus emphasizes Xerxes' responsibility for the devastating defeat of his armada. In his mother's dream (181-200), Greece and Persia appear as two quarreling sisters, whom Xerxes harnesses and yokes to his chariot. The Greek sibling rebels, smashing the yoke and causing Xerxes to fall. Atossa's nightmare alludes to Xerxes' spanning the straits that separate Asia from Europe (67-72, 128-32). He 'yoked the Hellespont' and 'closed up the great Bosporos' (722-3) on his way to Greece, then fled with few survivors 'back over the bridge that yoked the two continents' (736). Darius' ghost condemns Xerxes for thinking he could 'bind the sacred flowing Hellespont in shackles like a slave,/ and alter the divine flow of the Bosporos with hammered links of chain,/ .../ a mortal who would master all the gods,/ even Poseidon' (745-50). In his lust for expansion, Xerxes unites what the sea-god keeps apart, with catastrophic results. In effect, Xerxes breaks up his own kingdom, 'unyoking' the wedded couples of Persia (133-9, 287-9, 537-45), and tainting the seed in the earth: 'For *hubris* flowered forth and produced a crop of ruin,/ and from it reaped a harvest of endless tears' (821-2). Xerxes empties Persia of its natural growth: 'this flowering of men, nourished by the whole land of Asia, dead and gone' (59-62); 'the flower of Persia fallen, dead and gone' (252).

Xerxes' yoking the Hellespont serves the ends of imperialism, pure and simple. By bridging the continents, he hopes to forge the yoke of slavery on the Greeks and subject them to tyrannical rule. Their resistance leads to Xerxes' disaster, configured (like that of Capaneus, noted earlier) as a fall from high to low. On the way, Xerxes meets the power of the gods – in the elements of nature and their corresponding divinities, in the predictions of the deified Darius, and in the will of Zeus manifest in the military debacle. By insulting these forces, Xerxes overlooks a principle that the play is at pains to establish: when humans climb too high and reach too far, their fall is inevitable and cataclysmic, with effects that extend across the community at large.

In *Antigone*, Sophocles draws special attention to Creon's role in unleashing the tragic events. In Teiresias' speech, the blind prophet rebukes Creon for refusing Polyneices burial and for burying Antigone alive, both offences against the gods:

> You sent below one who belongs above,
> lodging a living soul dishonourably in a tomb,
> and you kept here one who belongs below, against
> the gods – a dispossessed, unmourned, unholy corpse.
>
> Sophocles *Antigone* 1068-71

Haimon, too, exposes Creon's responsibility for the disasters that occur. Focusing on politics rather than religion, he accuses his father of abrogating the rights of the citizens of Thebes. In their exchange, Creon reveals his autocratic view of political power, asking rhetorically whether he rules the city for himself or for others (736), and stating flat out that the city 'belongs to its ruler' (738). Haimon responds prophetically: 'You would rule well as a lone monarch in the desert' (739). As if turning his son's words against him, Creon condemns Antigone to be 'left alone and deserted' (887), an action – like exposing Polyneices' corpse – that brings ruin on Creon's city, his family, and himself.

In these examples, powerful protagonists fail to control their drive for dominance, wreaking havoc on the communities they represent. However, as we all know, tragedy does not respond solely to personal desires and actions. Escaping tragic disaster is not simply a matter of exercising self-control over *hubris* or showing humility before the cosmos. Human agency properly practised is *not* a sufficient condition for avoiding calamity, as we see in *Oedipus Tyrannus*, *Ajax*, *Trachiniae*, *Heracles*, *Ion*, and many other tragedies. Fate operates as its own agent, like a powerful electromagnet that draws everyone into its field, converting apparently independent choices and random circumstance into lines of causation that produce a tragic outcome.

Almost by definition, Greek tragedy relies on causalities beyond human agency. To put it differently, fate is the enabling circumstance that allows tragic events to take place. If human agency *were* all powerful, then moral psychomachia and melodrama – presenting, respectively, the internal and external battle between good and evil – would replace tragedy as *the* serious form of theatre. In both morality plays and melodramas, virtue and vice are clearly distinguished, and in the latter virtue always wins in the end. Tragedy is rarely so neat, as we see in *Antigone*. There nobody 'wins', for Creon's edict forbidding Polyneices' burial sets off a chain reaction, resulting in the suicides of Antigone, Haimon, and Eurydice, and the devastation of Creon himself. In Euripides' *Ion* the trajectory moves in the opposite direction, but the characters still find themselves enabled by fate. The voluntary actions of unrecognized mother and son nearly lead to Ion's murder of Creusa and Creusa's murder of Ion. However, the design of Apollo intervenes, reuniting Creusa and Ion, who face a future in Athens that differs radically from the prospects they once had imagined.

These examples confirm what critics from Aristotle onwards point out, namely that tragedy focuses on mutability and reversal (*peripeteia*). The direction of the change is not necessarily towards catastrophe, as people assume when they use the word 'tragedy' only for disastrous events. The interplay of human agency and fate can lead to surprising outcomes, some of which mark an extraordinary improvement on the previous situation. Although preferring plots that shift from good to bad fortune, like that of *Oedipus Tyrannus*, Aristotle also holds up Euripides' *Iphigenia among the Taurians* as a model tragedy. In this play, the dramatic situation moves from potential disaster to near-miraculous salvation.[31] After the recognition scene between Iphigenia and Orestes, they (along with Pylades) escape from the Thracian king Thoas and make their way home to Greece. Clearly, mutability *in itself* proved sufficiently interesting to the Greeks to warrant its ongoing representation on the tragic stage.

Given the central role of change and reversal in Greek tragedy, we should note that the underlying causes rarely take the oppositional form 'agency vs. fate', as in Christian discussions of free will and predestination, or in later debates on individual freedom vs. determinism (whether social, materialist, or biological). Tragedy offers a paradoxical combination of agency as fate, and fate as agency, as I suggest in the chapter title. Having begun with this dyad in tragedy, let us turn briefly to the 'fate' that human agency has suffered in recent analyses of power and authority.

In the academy, the legal profession, and in popular psychology, the notion of personal agency has come under intense scrutiny. The Enlightenment commitment to individual freedom and responsibility has given way to the discourse of power, emphasizing regimens of discipline, punishment and social control. Literary critics challenge the idea of personal authority and authorial origins (whether of books or of actions). Social scientists and psychologists focus on suffering and victimization, where passive endurance replaces active resistance. Historians eschew master narratives in which individual players exercise influence over social and economic forces. A belief in the reality of 'networks' and 'fields' undermines the prerogatives of individual responsibility, rejecting (in effect) Brecht's view that 'evil has a telephone number'. In the law courts, legal defences based on mitigating factors – hormones, junk food, childhood abuse, substance dependency, cultural influences, temporary insanity – claim that these pressures and forces become internalized and diminish responsibility. Something else *made it happen*. Or in the inimitable words of President Ronald Reagan, when asked about the Iran-Contra scandal, 'Mistakes were made' – but no one he knew made them.

The pervasive sense that there is no 'there' there frustrates our efforts to locate a party responsible for a specific act or state of affairs. Selves multiply within the psyche, making agency internally contingent and conflicted. The infinite play of the signifier posits that fixity of meaning is a naive mirage. Power structures in business and government – heavily promoted when the going is good – become hopelessly intricate and fugitive in times of trouble.[32] In the face of global crises, we witness the endless deferral of responsibility and decision making, as if time had no stop, and death (finally) never

comes. We might contrast the self-judgement of Oedipus, who –
through no fault of his own – commits horrific crimes:

> Hurl me out of this land, as fast as possible, where
> I might be in the company of no other human being.
> …
> For his [Apollo's] prophecy made it clear that I,
> killer of my father, should perish for my impiety.
> Sophocles Oedipus Tyrannus 1436-41[33]

Much of the current assault on personal choice and responsibility
reflects the accurate perception that individuals *per se* have little
influence over economic and social forces that shape their lives. In
capitalist economies, individual freedom is trumpeted in the market
place, as if atomized purchasing units could buy 'liberty'. In many
so-called democracies, voting (what passes for individual influence on
the political process) means ratifying decisions others have taken, or
choosing between candidates who represent the same interests. Gore
Vidal describes the United States as having 'one political party with
two right wings', a reality that extends to the United Kingdom with
'New Labour' (giving the UK *three* parties with a similar agenda). In
many cases, political freedom sinks to the level of 'demonstration
elections', Edward Herman's apt phrase for elections staged to prove
that a 'fledgling democracy' (US doublespeak for an obedient third-
world ally) has taken wing, making it eligible for renewed military
aid and arms sales.[34] In elections effectively controlled by big money,
the military, and the ruling elite, individual voting amounts to playing a game whose outcome (no matter who 'wins') is fixed in advance.
The gods in Greek tragedy appear weak by comparison.

Contemporary factors like these contribute to the sense that personal agency is an anachronism, a holdover from more idealistic
times that didn't understand the shaping operations of power and
'discourse'. Thinking through the issue, however, reveals a deeper
truth. Certainly, agency and self-determination are subject to powerful forces. But the concerted efforts at controlling what individuals
think and do – what Noam Chomsky and Edward Herman call 'the
manufacturing of consent' – would not be necessary if there weren't
real concerns over our potential freedom to think and act differently.

The presence of contemporary forms of social and ideological pressure proves that individual choice is potentially dangerous. It must be influenced, channelled, redirected, or repressed.[35] How Greek tragedy played into and resisted such forces in fifth-century Athens provides the subject of our next chapter, 'Tragedy and Ideology'.

With these observations in mind, let us return to the tragic question – *ti drasô*, 'What shall I do?' – and see how it draws agency and fate together in Sophocles' *Philoctetes*. Issues of choice and action drive the play, and particularly the character of Neoptolemus, the young warrior-son of Achilles who had recently been slain at Troy. Neoptolemus (whose name means 'new to war') accompanies the experienced Odysseus to the island of Lemnos, where the Greeks marooned their comrade Philoctetes ten years before because a suppurating leg-wound made his presence unbearable. Following a prophecy that Troy will fall only when Philoctetes and his bow rejoin the expedition, the Greek leaders send the two men on a mission to bring him back. Under Odysseus' influence, Neoptolemus abandons his principles of honesty and fair play to gain the confidence of the lonely hero, pretending that he will take Philoctetes home rather than to Troy.

At eight moments in the play, the 'tragic question' rings out like a cry in the dark. The first occasion follows Philoctetes' epileptic fit from the pain of his wound, prompting the shocked Neoptolemus to cry 'What shall I do?' [*ti drasô*]. Philoctetes responds, 'Don't tremble in fright and betray me' (757), meaning 'Don't abandon me when I collapse', but unconsciously suggesting Neoptolemus' fear of Odysseus and the treacherous abduction he has planned for Philoctetes. Here, a cry born of innocence and concern points to a darker truth, as if the reality of Philoctetes' physical pain could somehow unmask Neoptolemus' deception.

Before collapsing into a sickly sleep, Philoctetes entrusts Neoptolemus with his bow for safekeeping. Talismanic weapon in hand, Neoptolemus approaches his own moral crisis: 'Ahhh! What shall I do [*ti dêt' an drôim' egô*] now?' (895), he asks. Philoctetes thinks that his friend's unease arises from the noxious wound, but the disgust that Neoptolemus feels stems from his own behaviour: 'Everything is distasteful when a man abandons his own nature,/ and chooses to do what goes against the grain' (902-3). Earlier, Odysseus advised Neoptolemus to abandon his moral reservations: 'Now, for a few brief hours, give yourself/ over to me, and after that – for the rest of time –/ be known as the most reverent of all mortals' (83-5). Under Odysseus' guidance, Neoptolemus has done just that, insinuating himself into Philoctetes' confidence in order to abduct him to Troy.

Compelled by his honesty to divulge the real mission, Neoptolemus asks the tragic question a third time: 'Oh Zeus, what shall I do? [*ti drasô*]. Will I prove doubly villainous/ for having hidden what I have to say and now for saying what is shameful?' (908-9). Learning the truth from Neoptolemus, Philoctetes begs not to be forced to go to Troy and serve the very men who had abandoned him. Moved by his appeal, the Chorus of Greek sailors ask Neoptolemus what he has been asking himself: 'What shall we do [*ti drômen*]?' (963). Confronted on all sides by his own duplicity, Neoptolemus responds for the fifth time with the cry of conflicted agency: 'Oh no, what shall I do [*ti drasô*]? If only I had never left/ [my home] Skyros, so awful is the situation I find myself in' (969-70). At this point, Neoptolemus longs for the innocence he had known before joining the Greek expedition, and as he prepares to grant Philoctetes' request, he asks his comrades one last time, 'What shall we do [*ti drômen*], men?' (974).

Until this point in the play, Neoptolemus faces a choice between official (albeit cruel and duplicitous) duty to the Greek army, and truth to his own conscience. The choice resembles that of Agamemnon at Aulis, where the hero is torn between his duty as commander of the Greek fleet and his love for his own daughter. However, in *Agamemnon*, the anger of the goddess Artemis makes the dilemma seem far more externally determined than in *Philoctetes*, where the gods seem distant and uninvolved. Unlike Agamemnon, Neoptolemus hesitates because of his growing compassion for Philoctetes and his disgust at betraying him to the instrumental uses of the Greeks. A victim of self-alienation, Neoptolemus gives every indication of abandoning the mission and committing himself to help a miserable fellow-human find his way home.

Sophocles temporarily takes the decision out of Neoptolemus' hands by having Odysseus arrive unexpectedly to halt any further failure of resolve. Odysseus seizes the bow – Philoctetes' sole means of survival – and leaves with Neoptolemus, apparently off to Troy.

Abandoned on Lemnos a second time, Philoctetes now asks the tragic question of himself: 'What shall I do [*ti drasô*]' (1063). The cry is desperate, for Philoctetes – unlike Neoptolemus – has no control over events. Deceived by the young man he had trusted and deprived of his bow by Odysseus, Philoctetes faces certain death, with no means of hunting or protecting himself, and with no hope of seeing his home again.

A further Sophoclean twist occurs when Neoptolemus returns unexpectedly and gives the bow back to Philoctetes, over Odysseus' vehement objections. Although repeating the offer to take him home, Neoptolemus tries once more to persuade Philoctetes to accompany him to Troy, promising eternal glory at the city's fall and a cure for his infected wound. With renewed faith in Neoptolemus, Philoctetes finds himself torn between his hope that the young man's promises are true, and his deep hatred of the Greeks – particularly Odysseus – who have treated him so mercilessly. For the last time the tragic question rings out, but now it is Philoctetes who must choose: 'What shall I do [*ti drasô*]?' (1350).

The play seems to answer the question at the level of human agency. Neoptolemus chooses to follow his own moral sense, and, consistent with his earlier wishes, Philoctetes decides to sail home to his family, leaving the Trojan quagmire to the Greeks he loathes. In a stunning *coup de théâtre*, however, Sophocles turns these decisions on their head. Out of the blue, the deified Heracles appears on high, telling Philoctetes to sail with Neoptolemus and Odysseus to Troy. There he will use the bow (originally a gift from Heracles) to capture the city, and he also will find a cure for his disease. The appearance of Heracles *ex machina* complicates the notion of purely human agency, for the workings of fate assert themselves via divine inter-vention and imperative. Troy is doomed to fall; Philoctetes must play his role in that event; the legends of the war and homecoming of the Greeks depend on the outcome; myth, history, and the gods require an ending different from what the individual characters might choose for themselves.

Does this mean that Heracles' appearance undermines human agency or invalidates the tragic question? Perhaps not, as Heracles' closing admonition suggests:

3. The Fate of Agency, the Agency of Fate

... But keep this firmly in mind, when you
conquer the land: reverence all that concerns the gods.
All else is secondary to the great father, Zeus.
For such reverence does not die along with mortals;
whether humans live or pass away, it is never destroyed.

Sophocles *Philoctetes* 1440-4

Heracles alludes to the horrors that the Greeks will perpetrate at the sack of Troy, none more infamous than Neoptolemus' slaughter of the suppliant King Priam at the altar of Zeus, a scene frequently depicted on Attic vases. Heracles' pointed warning reminds both the characters and the audience of the crucial interplay of agency, choice, self-control, and respect for the realm of the gods. That Neoptolemus – in the myth, if not yet in Sophocles' play – becomes a heartless butcher at Troy indicates the truth of Thucydides' dictum that 'war is a harsh teacher'. It also points to the need for humans to make full use of their free agency even as they are held in the hands of fate.

In the end, we – much like the Greeks – confront a secular version of Pascal's Wager. We can choose to believe that we have no influence over events, no significant decisions to make, that we have been programmed from within, that we face immovable forces from without, that these things guarantee the world is the way it is, no matter what we may think or do about it. The problem with this view, as Noam Chomsky points out, is that it remains hopelessly self-fulfilling. If we act on the belief that we have no influence on the world that shapes us, then we ensure that we will have no effect on it, precisely what those who hold the reins of power would like us to believe.[36]

Let us pretend for a moment that the following (highly suspect) assumptions are true: human beings are selfish genes run amok; the territorial imperative dominates human history; males are violent and aggressive by nature; greed is hard-wired into the species; divine sanction and manifest destiny belong to these people but not to their neighbours; a twist of fate can dictate that you will kill your father and marry your mother. Should we then race to fulfil these social, biological, economic, or supernatural 'facts', unleashing greed, seizing power, maximizing aggression, killing whenever and whomever we 'must'?

Clearly this scenario has little to recommend it. Whatever restrictions operate on us, we face the human necessity to act as if our actions mattered, without blaming it on fate, genes, or 'them'. Of course, we can (and should) offer an alternative view of human nature, one amply illustrated in Greek tragedy, where solidarity, sympathy, cooperation, and the instinct for freedom and self-sacrifice are prominent features. Finally, when facing the tragic question *ti drasô*, we can do anything we like but refuse to answer it. Human limits are the basis of what freedom we have, and Greek tragedy allows us to engage that paradox without closing our eyes or running the other way.

4

Tragedy and Ideology

For in no way do the gods put up
with hubris.

Sophocles *Women of Trachis* 280

Be all you can be
in the US Army.

US Army recruiting jingle, 2002

Questionable assumptions

In the last two chapters we have dealt with Greek tragedy's response
to fear, and to the paradoxical interactions of agency and fate. Drawing them together, we might say that tragedy locates its characters
in frightening, high-stakes situations for which they bear more or
less responsibility, and then demands that they act. The Greek word
for this predicament, *krisis*, does not indicate breakdown or chaos –
as in our word 'crisis' – but rather implies a choice or decision. Facing
a critical situation, individuals in a community are subject to numer-
ous influences, including previous models of appropriate behaviour.
We might call the matrix of these influences 'ideology', the nexus of
basic assumptions that members of a society hold (or are expected to
hold), into which they are educated or indoctrinated, and for which
they are rewarded. Under normal circumstances, ideology goes un-
noticed or unchallenged, providing the underlying (and frequently
unexamined) basis for opinion, belief, and action.[1]

In times of crisis, people tend to draw on these templates of
thought and action, validating the very ideology that informs their
reaction. However, when events become sufficiently severe or trau-
matic (as those in Greek tragedy usually are), people can challenge
these assumptions, breaking through the normal constraints on

87

understanding and response. In this way, extreme circumstances open up new ways of thinking and acting, generating new *kriseis* (choices) that might transform and even undermine ideological regimes.

Let us illustrate this possibility by tracking the United States' response to the terrorist attacks on the World Trade Center and Pentagon in September 2001. Americans expressed reactions ranging from disbelief to anger, shock to grief, patriotism to racism, courage to fear. For the first time in almost two centuries, the United States experienced large-scale, foreign-perpetrated violence on its own soil aimed (mainly) at civilians.[2] By virtue of its uniqueness and devastation, the attack of 9/11 opened up a space in American society that had not been there before. Now *we* knew what other countries and peoples had experienced – violent death out of the blue, unexpected, unconscionable, and undeniable.

The events of 9/11 momentarily forced the United States to confront violence from the perspective of the *victims* of terror. Almost immediately, however, that reaction was replaced by the sanctioned ideology of patriotism and militarism, a response that unleashed more death and destruction on the innocent.[3] Coordinated and disseminated by powerful government and corporate institutions, an avalanche effectively silenced other voices and responses. When these voices could be heard (in the alternative press, at protests, among a number of activist and interest groups), they spoke of a deep sympathy for the victims of terror, including the terrorism committed by the US and its clients.

Other reactions in this vein included criticism of US military preparedness and the assumptions on which it was based;[4] doubts about US foreign policy, the source of much hatred and contempt abroad;[5] and a re-evaluation of previous US involvement in Afghanistan, including military support for the Mujahadin, many of whom later formed the Taliban (the Afghan government whom the Bush administration turned into the equivalent of al-Qaeda). Alternatives to the official story challenged the power of US oil interests, including oil-pipeline plans for Afghanistan, and US support for undemocratic oil-producing states in the Middle East and elsewhere. Several studies re-examined the interlocking connections between international 'development', foreign investment, and cheap labour, recalling President Dwight Eisenhower's warning some forty years ago about 'the gravest danger posed to our democratic government, the military-industrial complex'.[6]

Before such reactions could find their way to the wider public, however, the US government called for retribution and revenge, a cry echoed by Congress, the corporate media, and the usual group-think intellectuals. The President declared a 'war on terrorism', asserting that those not for the war were the enemy. Urged by the administration, Congress authorized an unprecedented increase in the US defence budget, and passed various 'anti-terrorist' laws that threaten civil rights formerly guaranteed to US citizens and anyone on American soil. Other violations of the US Constitution were deemed unimportant, including Congress' power to declare war (Article I, Section 8). The Bush Administration rejected out of hand Taliban offers to hand Osama bin Laden over to a third-party (World Court, United Nations) on the presentation of evidence linking him to the attacks. Instead, the President and Secretary of Defense announced a bounty of $1,000,000 for bin Laden 'dead or alive', as if the country had found itself in a John Ford western. And the US mounted a large-scale military campaign to overthrow the government of Afghanistan (a country that most Americans can neither spell nor locate on a map), making no effort to determine who among the Taliban authorities knew about or condoned the 9/11 attacks.[7]

With massive bombing and some ground support, the US and its ally Great Britain re-empowered the Northern Alliance, a mishmash of competing warlords who previously had ruled Afghanistan (1992-96) so violently and corruptly that the Taliban offered relative (albeit repressive) peace and security.[8] As relief agencies begged for funds to stop a humanitarian disaster, billions were dedicated to the ongoing military action, including a spree of new US military bases to be built in Afghanistan, Uzbekistan, Turkmenistan and Tajikistan. US troops prepared for military operations in the Philippines, Georgia, Yemen and Somalia, and officials soberly insisted on plans to overthrow the governments of Iraq, Iran and North Korea (occasionally throwing in Cuba, for old times' sake), countries that constituted – according to President Bush – an 'axis of evil'. Icing the ideological cake, the President assured one and all that the US was 'open for business', urging all good citizens to shop, while American flags became so popular that sweatshops in China had to work overtime to meet the demand.

The fact that few aspects of this story made the news or entered public debate within the United States suggests that ideology served its function well. The 9/11 crisis unleashed a highly coordinated, well funded, and extremely effective response, filling this new bottle with the same old wine. As one might have predicted, the 'war on terrorism' has secured a burgeoning military budget and greater concentration of power in the executive branch. A loosely defined, permanent state of hostilities allows for the repression of local dissidents and political resistance not only in the United States, but across the globe: Chechens by the Russians, Palestinians by the Israelis, leftist rebels (and unarmed union organizers) by the Colombian military and their paramilitary death squads, Kurds by the Turks, Tibetans by the Chinese, independence movements in Aceh and Irian Jaya by the government of Indonesia, human rights activists by governments throughout the Third Word, and so on. Making the world 'safe' from terror has meant sanctioning a massive increase in state-sponsored terrorism against already dispossessed and subjugated peoples, silencing legitimate questions about internal power and the ideology that sustains it.[9]

With this contemporary example in mind, let us return to the society that gave us Greek tragedy. Fifth-century Athens had its own dominant modes of thought, providing interesting points of comparison with our own. Buoyed by early political and military successes, the Athenian *polis* developed a strong civic ideology that balanced the traditional power of elite families with the democratic protocols of citizen participation. Democracy in Athens proved quick-rooted and resilient, surviving an array of perils and disasters: the Persian invasions of 490 and 480-479; the reluctance of Greek cities to join the Athenian alliance against the Persians and serve the emerging empire of Athens; the long Peloponnesian War (431-404) during which the Spartan enemy occupied Attica, allied cities revolted, and Athens eventually lost her empire; the two oligarchic coups of 411 and 404 (the latter after Sparta's victory), neither of which successfully supplanted popular rule in the long run; and the daily tensions between citizens of different classes, and among male citizens, women, metics (resident aliens), and slaves. Radical democracy in

Athens hung on until 322, a run of 185 years, which includes significant spans both before and after the Athenian empire.

What role did Attic tragedy play in developing, inculcating, or challenging democratic ideology? As noted in Chapter 1, scholars have emphasized the democratic roots of ancient theatre, viewing it less as a site for spectators interested in dramatic performances (the way we imagine theatre today) and more as a place for Athenian citizens to celebrate their city's status and accomplishments at a state-sponsored festival. At the City Dionysia, for example, pre-performance ceremonies in the orchestra included the presentation of the allies' tribute (in the days of the Delian League and Athenian empire); a parade of hoplite-armed war-orphans on their eighteenth birthday, who had been reared at the city's expense; the public announcement of manumitted slaves, involving the audience as potential legal witnesses (before written contracts came into use in the fourth century); and the presentation of various civic honours.

Also at the City Dionysia, intra-city competitions in the dithyramb, a form of choral poetry performed by a chorus of fifty, pitted Attica's ten tribes (*phylê*) against one another. Each tribe entered two choruses, one of men and one of boys, a process that helped build group identity within the *phylê*, a conglomerate of non-proximate villages that Cleisthenes introduced in the democratic revolution of 508/7. These new political divisions helped shift loyalties from traditional familial and local ties to a broader sense of the democratic community.

It is important to note, however, that tragic and comic competitions at the City Dionysia differed significantly from the pre-performance ceremonies and the dithyrambic contests. Based on its form and its mythological content, tragedy developed broad panhellenic appeal. Although the producers (wealthy Athenians drafted by the city) and the chorus members had to be Athenian citizens, the playwrights, actors, and *aulos* accompanists frequently were non-Athenian. As noted in Chapter 1, the audience came from many parts of Greece, not just Athens, and the eclectic form of tragedy incorporated many influences and regional variations, including Doric forms for lyric and Ionic for dramatic speech. The spoken sections show the influence of Athenian public debate (in the assembly and council), legal argumentation (in the lawcourts), encomiastic praise (funeral orations over the dead), and the rhetoric of the sophists (at private symposia, or in the *agora*). Tragic lyric drew from a variety of sources, including ritual songs for weddings and funerals, paeans to Apollo, hymns to Zeus, songs in praise of Dionysus, and prayers to Artemis. Throughout the plays, one hears the echo of earlier performances of Homer, the lyric poets, and other playwrights. The ancient theatre had a reciprocal effect on these sources, suggesting a complicated relationship between tragedy and Athenian ideology.

When we get to the individual tragedies, something even more remarkable emerges. We do find speeches, characters, and situations that endorse misogyny, slavery, political violence, imperial ruthlessness, and Athenian propaganda. But far more frequently we find these subjects presented from the point of view of their victims. We meet abused wives (Deianeira, Medea, Phaedra, Clytemnestra, Eurydice) and daughters (Electra, Iphigenia, Antigone); captive or enslaved women (the Danaids, Tecmessa, Iole and the women of Oechalia, the Dionysus-possessed women of Thebes); the targets of power and political expediency (Prometheus, Philoctetes, Neoptolemus, the exiled Orestes, Megara, Amphitryon, the sons of Heracles); the casualties of war (Hecuba, Andromache, Cassandra, Polyxena, the women of Troy). Their prominence constitutes an inbuilt criticism of various Athenian practices and assumptions, making tragic performance an unsettling public act.

The potential for challenging ideological norms reflects tragedy's size and scale, its complex and catholic form, the polyphony of competing dramatic voices, the archetypal appeal of its mythological frame, the festival license granted by the City, and the fact that productions took place out-of-doors before a large audience.[10] Greek tragedy, at least in the fifth century, presented alternative voices of undeniable power. By having those voices bound to a narrative of the mythic past, tragedians avoided overt topicality. However, this does not mean they simply championed or strengthened Athens' self-image. As we shall see, how effectively they challenged the dominant ideology is not only a matter of Greek cultural and political history, but also a test of our own theatrical and critical response.

4. Tragedy and Ideology

Patriarchy and male domination

No aspect of Greek tragedy has been more contentious in recent years than its relationship to patriarchy and male domination. Generally speaking, men have held physical, social, political, economic, and legal power over women across much of the globe for most of recorded history. Fifth-century Athens was no exception. Some scholars, however, think that Athens represented the apogee of patriarchy and misogyny among societies of the ancient Mediterranean, a dubious claim given that we know so much more about Athens than other cities in the same period. Greek tragedy certainly offers an array of characters who are sexist, gynophobic or misogynist: Aeschylus' Apollo (*Eumenides*) and the Egyptian cousins (*Suppliant Women*); Sophocles' Heracles (*Women of Trachis*), Ajax (*Ajax*), and Creon (*Antigone*); Euripides' Jason (*Medea*), Hippolytus (*Hippolytus*), and Pentheus (*Bacchae*). Although not punished directly for their behaviour toward women, these characters do come to particularly bad ends. Ajax kills himself on a desolate beach; Creon unintentionally prompts the suicide of his son and wife and is left a broken man; Jason suffers the deaths of his new bride, her father, and his own two sons; Hippolytus dies after being mangled on the rocky shoreline, dragged by his team of horses; and Pentheus is torn apart by the Dionysus-crazed women of Thebes, including his own mother.

As well as portraying chauvinists who come to grief, tragedy presents remarkable female characters who challenge male power and patriarchy. Sophocles' Antigone and Electra demonstrate women's capacity for heroic resistance, in contrast to their sisters Ismene and Chrysothemis, and to the population at large. The Danaids stand up to male domination by committing murder in Aeschylus' *Suppliant Women*, as does Medea (for different reasons) in *Medea*. As discussed in Chapter 2, the Chorus of Oceanids in *Prometheus Bound* prefer to die in solidarity with Prometheus than to live under the tyranny of Zeus. Aethra in Euripides' *Suppliant Women* breaks her self-imposed silence and intervenes in a crucial (and deadly) area of civic policy, persuading her son Theseus to fight for the Hellenic norm of burying the dead.

Even in the direst of straits, female tragic characters respond with dignity and courage. Sacrificed at Achilles' tomb by the Greek army, the Trojan princess Polyxena in *Hecuba* takes imaginative control over her death, asserting what little power she has to its full effect. Her sister Cassandra in *Agamemnon* displays heart-rending courage as she meets her death in the house of Atreus. Although their circumstances differ, Alcestis and Tecmessa demonstrate similar strength of will in the face of doom, putting their respective husbands Admetus and Ajax to shame.

As well as presenting 'an array of female characters unprecedented in their variety',[11] tragedy also 'feminizes' many of its male heroes. After his heroic battle to recover the Argive dead in *Suppliant Women*, Theseus shows remarkable restraint in refusing to sack the fallen city of Thebes. Instead of pursuing his military advantage, he bathes and prepares for burial the corpses he has recovered, an 'unmanly' act traditionally performed by women. Allowing his mother to affect public policy, avoiding violent excess in victory, and assuming the female role in death ritual, Theseus emerges as a new kind of leader, 'the kind of general one should choose' (726), the Messenger asserts. Here Euripides brings together fictional and real worlds, alluding to the democratic election of Athenian generals that took place each year shortly after the City Dionysia.

In Euripides' *Alcestis*, Admetus realizes what his wife means to him only after she dies in his place: 'I learn too late' (*arti manthanô* 940). By the end of the play, Admetus finds himself submitting to the male authority of his friend Heracles, who forces him to accept a 'new' spouse he does not choose for himself. In so doing, Admetus assumes the female role in the protocols of a normal Greek wedding. In *Women of Trachis*, Sophocles presents Heracles as a victim of destructive eros, typically a female experience in Greek myth. Screaming in agony when he appears onstage, Heracles suffers just like a woman, condemned to weakness and pain rarely associated with a male hero:

> ... Pity me,
> pitiable for so many reasons, for now I weep and cry
> like a girl. Never before could anyone say
> he saw me, a man, behave in such a fashion.
> Without tears I always endured what evil befell me.
> But now torment has shown me as a wretched woman.
> Sophocles *Women of Trachis* 1070-5

94

In similar fashion, at the end of Euripides' *Heracles* the protagonist finds himself led towards Athens by Theseus 'like a little boat in tow' (*HF* 1423-6), the same image used when Heracles rescues his wife and children from the tyrant Lycus and leads them to apparent safety (*HF* 631-6). The tragic reversals of the play force Heracles to become dependent on a male hero, the sort of figure he himself once epitomized. In a different vein, Menelaus in Euripides' *Helen* maintains a macho image, preferring death to the shame of asking for mercy and admitting his own powerlessness. Meanwhile his wife Helen secures a reprieve and plans their successful escape (*Hel.* 947-95, 1032-92). Even when tragic heroes behave 'like men', their female counterparts frequently prove more intelligent, efficacious, and sympathetic.

In 20 of the 32 extant tragedies, the Chorus consist of women, originally played by Athenian citizens. Taking on the roles of female captives, slaves, and victims of male violence, male performers expanded their own imaginary experience, as well of those of the (primarily) male audience, a process analysed by Froma Zeitlin and Helene Foley.[12] The prominence of this phenomenon in tragedy suggests that the genre challenged male patriarchy as much as it reinforced it. In its presentation of female characters, Greek tragedy effectively and unsentimentally embodies the insight of the English historian R.H. Tawney: 'Sympathy is a form of knowledge'.[13]

Slaves and female captives

On seeing the newly captured women brought to her *oikos* ('household') as Heracles' war booty, Deianeira in Sophocles' *Women of Trachis* responds with compassion verging on the subversive:

How can I fail to rejoice, hearing of my husband's
triumphant success evidenced here?
It is right for my joy to match his.
Nevertheless, those who think things through
fear [*tarbein*] for the man who succeeds, lest fortune trip him up.
Friends, a strange pity comes over me
when I see these wretched women, homeless,
fatherless, adrift in a foreign land.
Once, perhaps, they were daughters of free men,

but now they live the lives of slaves.
Zeus, lord of reversals [or 'turning points', *tropaie*],
may you never attack my offspring in this way .../ .../
Such is my fear [*dedoika*] when I see these women.
[to Iole] Unhappy one, of the maidens here who are you?
Have you no husband? Are you a mother? You seem
out of place, inexperienced in this, a princess perhaps.
.../ Who is her mother? What man fathered her?
Tell me, for I pitied her most as soon as I saw her,
insofar as a woman alone can feel and understand.

Sophocles Women of Trachis 293-313

Observing Greek proprieties, Deianeira puts her husband's victory first, but her speech reveals her conflicted emotions. She moves from fearing the reversals of fortune that the enslaved women embody to feeling outright pity for them in their captive state. Deianeira then focuses on a single individual [Iole] for whom she feels particular sympathy, as a woman alone herself. A speech that begins with male triumph ends with an expression of female solidarity with its victims.

Deianeira and Iole are both casualties of Heracles' erotic passion. Learning that her husband sacked Oechalia in order to seize Iole as his concubine, Deianeira does not humiliate her rival, as one might expect (compare Clytemnestra's treatment of Cassandra in *Agamemnon*, or Hermione's of Andromache in *Andromache*). Rather, Deianeira tries to regain Heracles' affection by using a love-potion that (unknown to her) is a poison, leading to her husband's death and her own suicide. Reversals abound in *Women of Trachis*, but – as Deianeira fears when she sees the captive women – they affect those who have triumphed as well as those who have suffered defeat. That the reversals operate within a context of female fellow-feeling may serve to question the patriarchal order and its assumptions about women.

Sophocles plants the seed for Deianeira's sympathetic response to Iole in an early exchange with her Nurse, a domestic slave:

Nurse: My mistress, Deianeira, how often before
have I seen you bewail Heracles' absence,
weeping your heart out in grief.
But now, if a slave may give advice

96

to those who are free, then I must speak ...
Deianeira: ... words even from the low-born
can hit the mark. This woman here is a slave,
but all she says is spoken by a free mind.
Sophocles Women of Trachis 49-53, 61-3

Deianeira recognizes that advice depends on the quality of what is said, not on the class or status of the speaker. Her sentiments anticipate those of the old Tutor in Euripides' *Ion*:

> There is only one thing that brings shame to slaves,
> the name. In all other things a slave (provided
> he's a good person) is no more base than a free man.
Euripides Ion 854-6

The Chorus of slave women in *Ion* prove the truth of this observation. They risk their own deaths to tell their Queen of her husband Xuthus' plan to introduce an interloper into the palace as their 'son'.[14] Here, as in *Women of Trachis*, solidarity within the household and between women challenges the boundaries of slave and free.

Like Iole, Tecmessa in Sophocles' *Ajax* is a war-prize, slave, and concubine. However, she lives with her captor as his wife and the mother of his son. Recovering from his humiliating madness, Ajax thinks of ending his life, prompting Tecmessa to deliver a speech that echoes Andromache's plea to Hector in *Iliad* Book 6. Tecmessa reminds her husband of all she has suffered, urging him to follow her example and endure his present misfortune:

> My lord Ajax, there is no greater evil for humans
> than fate [*tuchê*] imposed by necessity.
> I was born of a free father,
> the wealthiest man in all of Phrygia,
> but now I am a slave. Thus it was settled by the gods,
> and – above all – by your own strength. As a result
> I share your bed and think well of you.
> I beg you, by Zeus who protects the hearth,
> and by your own bed where you and I have joined,
> do not let me suffer hurtful words from

your enemies, abandoning me to their uses.
If you die, and by dying abandon me,
know that on that day I will be taken
violently by the Greeks and live out
a slave's life along with your son.
...
There is no one else for me to look to
other than you. You annihilated my country in war,
and another fate [*moira*] dragged my mother and father
down to Hades, to dwell among the dead.
What country, what means of support are
open to me? My only safety lies in you.
Hold me in your thoughts, for surely a man
should remember the pleasure that has come his way.
A grace given should beget another, always.
But if a man lets the memory of those gifts
slip away, then his good name goes with them.

Sophocles Ajax 485-99, 514-24

Tecmessa has suffered humiliation, powerlessness and violation far worse than Ajax, and she faces an even bleaker future (along with her son) if Ajax fails to ward off impending disaster. Forced into marriage, with no choice in the matter and no path of escape, Tecmessa learns to make the best of things, to embrace her circumstance, to love the man and their child, and to struggle against a desperate future. Her instinct for survival is both realistic and noble, and Ajax's refusal to meet his own *peripeteia* with comparable courage and resilience looks like failure. In *Ajax*, a slave woman emerges as wiser and more admirable than her heroic husband, whose shame and self-pity all but blind him to those who serve, love, and depend on him.

Warfare and militarism

Among tragedy's many challenges to accepted modes of Athenian thought, the treatment of female slaves looms large. Given that males captured in war usually were killed, and the women and children enslaved by their conquerors, tragedy frequently associates women and slaves with warfare. In the post-Trojan War plays of

4. Tragedy and Ideology

Euripides (*Hecuba*, *Trojan Women*, *Andromache*), captive females provide the emotional core of the drama. Not only do they embody the arbitrary nature of slavery, but they denounce the violence against women and children that it represents. In *Hecuba*, the Greeks sacrifice Hecuba's daughter Polyxena at the grave of their dead hero Achilles. As Hecuba points out, this perverse ritual violates reason, law, religious practice, and basic Greek values:

> What necessity compelled them to human sacrifice
> at a tomb, where offering a bull is more fitting?
> Or if Achilles wanted to pay back those who slew him,
> how is it just for him to murder her?
> She never worked any harm against him.
> ...
> I make my case on the grounds of justice.
> ...
> Do not tear away my child from my arms; do not
> cut her down. Enough have been killed already.
> ...
> Those who exercise power must not use it wrongly
> nor think that their good fortune will last forever.
> I myself was once such a person, but no longer;
> a single day ripped away all my happiness.
> ...
> In your country you have a law against shedding blood,
> the same for slaves as for the free ...
>
> Euripides Hecuba 260-92

The fact that the army sacrifices Polyxena in spite of Hecuba's arguments suggests the chasm between the ideals of the Greeks and their actions, a disturbing aspect of the play that gathers momentum during its performance.

Trojan Women works in much the same way. Having killed all adult Trojan males, the Greeks prepare to sail, taking the Trojan women back to Greece as their slaves. Swayed by Odysseus' speech in an assembly, the Greek army decides to hurl Andromache's young son Astyanax from the battlements of Troy before razing the city to the ground. The responses of Andromache and Hecuba are echoed in the cries of contemporary victims of male terror, from the 'Mothers of the Disappeared' in Central and South America to the victims of Indonesian violence in East Timor:

> *Andromache*: Greeks, discoverers of evils beyond the barbaric,
> why kill this child who is guilty of nothing?
> ...
> Take him, drag him, hurl him, if that's what
> you want, then eat his flesh ...
> <div align="right">Euripides <i>Trojan Women</i> 764-5, 774-5</div>

> *Hecuba*: You sacked our city, you killed all the Trojans,
> yet you feared this little child. Damn such fear,
> and all who fear with no basis in thought or reason.
> ...
>   ... What epitaph
> would some poet write on your tomb for the ages?
> 'This small child lying here
> the famed Greeks killed out of fear'
> – words of lasting shame for Greece.
> <div align="right">Euripides <i>Trojan Women</i> 1164-6, 1188-91</div>

In this extraordinary play, Trojan 'barbarians' – the Greek term for non-Greek speakers – expose the barbarity of the Greeks. It is they who practise cruelty on the innocent, act with irrational paranoia, and lack any sense of human proportion. Hecuba's reference to the imaginary poet of Astyanax' epitaph recalls that art can record what history forgets. Reflexively it points to Euripides himself, whose play forces fifth-century Athenians to confront (indirectly) their own brutality.

Only a few months before the premiere of *Trojan Women*, in the midst of the Peloponnesian War, Athens invaded the island of Melos, killed the adult males, enslaved the women and children, and settled the depopulated island with Athenian colonists. According to Thucydides, Athens could no longer abide Melian neutrality, perceiving it as a threat to the empire. The Athenians argue that they have no choice but to squash Melos, given that power must protect itself and that 'might is right'.[15] In *Trojan Women*, under the guise of dramatizing mythic Greek barbarity, Euripides exposes the ideology of the

4. Tragedy and Ideology

Athenian empire and the butchery that sustains it. A contemporary parallel might involve Britain's National Theatre or its (hypothetical) American counterpart mounting a play in 1999 that showed the effects of the NATO bombing on Serbia (*unleashing* the refugee problem it ostensibly aimed to stop),[16] or dramatizing the plight of 'Taliban' prisoners and Afghan refugees today.

Euripides had no monopoly on tragedies that challenge the ideology of war, in part because warfare was a basic reality of Greek life. The Chorus of Aeschylus' *Agamemnon* forcefully convey the effects of foreign wars on the women forced to stay behind:

> For each man who sailed from Greece
> a woman sits in tears,
> her heart cut deep
> home after home.
> She knows the one she sent off,
> but takes back home
> an urn of ashes
> instead of a man.
> Ares [god of war] is the money-changer of bodies;
> his balance rests on the point of a spear.
> From the fires of Troy
> he sends dust that weighs heavy,
> soaked with the tears of loved ones.
> Urns swollen with ashes
> take the place of a man.
>
> Aeschylus *Agamemnon* 429-44

Clytemnestra also speaks of the anguish that a wife endures while waiting at home. Although her purpose may be deception, her speech rings with a lived truth:

> Cut off from her husband, a woman sits alone
> in the house, her sole companion – fear.
> Rumours break out like a plague, as messenger
> follows messenger, each with news worse than before,
> screaming their sorrow on the house.
>
> Aeschylus *Agamemnon* 861-5

In the same vein, Clytemnestra paints a verbal picture of the sack of Troy from the point of view of the conquered:

> Trojan women fall on the bodies of their dead,
> their husbands and brothers, and children
> cling to the corpses of their fathers. But the wails
> for the dead now come from the throats of slaves.
> Aeschylus *Agamemnon* 326-9

As for the conquerors, the Herald emphasizes the hardships they faced, anticipating the horrors of the Great War of the last century:

> We slept under the walls of the enemy's city.
> From the sky a steady drizzle worked on us,
> and, when it broke, the meadow dew rotting our clothes,
> and everywhere lice – our hair, our beards.
> And I could tell you of winter that slaughtered birds,
> the unbearable snow from Mount Ida,
> and the heat in summer, when waves melted
> and calm seized the exhausted sea.
> Aeschylus *Agamemnon* 559-66

Such reactions to the privations of war do not challenge the ideology of warfare *per se*. However, they do demonstrate tragedy's interest in exploring the underside of state-sponsored militarism, otherwise represented (both then and now) as intrinsically noble and heroic.

In Sophocles' *Ajax* we hear an outright rejection of war and those responsible for it. Although Ajax's reputation rests on hand-to-hand combat on land, Sophocles makes the Chorus of his companions *sailors* from Salamis, an island just off the coast of Attica and part of the Athenian *polis*. This group of sailors calls to mind the Athenian navy, and it significant that they sing a condemnation of war:

> How long? When will it end,
> the final count of wandering years?
> They bring on us a ceaseless blizzard

of spears and suffering
spread over the fields of Troy,
mournful shame to all the Greeks.
That man who invented war,
why didn't the sky open, or Hades
sink him in its common grave?
He showed Greeks how to fight, using common
weapons of hate, with war spawning war.
That man murdered humanity.
...

What joy, delight remains for us now?
If only we were at the forest headland,
approaching the sea-washed crag
of Sounion! There
we could greet again
holy Athens.

Sophocles Ajax 1185-98, 1215-22

The sailors curse the inventor of war, suggesting that the Greeks distinguished destructive tendencies within individuals from collective military violence. This passage anticipates pacifist arguments that differentiate individual aggression (a natural part of human experience) from violence organized by the state, involving professional armies, military hierarchies, the massing of armaments and matériel, and the propaganda needed to sustain the enterprise. The Chorus' desire to leave the battlefield for home echoes wherever soldiers find themselves fighting on foreign soil. But the fact that the sailors' home is *Athens* had special relevance for the original audience, reflecting their city's imperial position. The Chorus of sailors point to Athens in more ways than one.

In *Helen*, Euripides underlines his anti-war message by revealing the 'phantom' causes of the campaign on which the play – and much Greek mythology – depends, namely the Trojan War. Adopting Stesichorus' version of the story, Euripides has the Greeks wage the war over an ersatz Helen, an effigy sent to Troy by Zeus, who had whisked the real Helen off to Egypt. It is in this context that the Chorus cry out against the madness of war:

103

Fools, all who would win glory
by war and the spear's cutting edge,
senselessly you try to end
the burdens of humanity by killing.
If contests of blood are to settle
human conflict, then hateful strife
will never leave the cities of men.

Euripides Helen 1151-7

Consisting of maidens from Sparta, Athens' enemy in the Peloponnesian War, the Chorus (played by Athenian males) claim that war perpetuates violence rather than resolving conflicts. Their comments had special relevance in 412, when Euripides' play was first performed. Athens had just suffered a terrible defeat in Sicily, with its fleet destroyed and many Athenians held captive and imprisoned after the disastrous expedition against the allies of Sparta on the island (discussed further in Chapter 5).

In *Helen*, the cause of hostilities proves to be a literal fabrication, imposed from above. In Aeschylus' *Agamemnon*, however, the Chorus deal with the problematic origins of war on the human level. They contrast the concerns of the elite who lead the masses into battle with the suffering of the common people who must endure its consequences. Characterizing war in violent commercial terms ('a money-changer of bodies', quoted above), the Chorus describe how ordinary Greeks move from grief to anger against those who started the conflict 'for another man's [Menelaus'] wife' (*Agamemnon* 448):

Grief spreads its anger at the sons
of Atreus, those 'champions of justice'.
The walls of Troy like gravestones,
lovely bodies in hated soil
forever hold the land they won.
Etched with wrath, the people's voice
utters a curse that must be paid.
...
The gods are not blind
to the killers of many.
In time the Furies grind them down,

those who prosper unjustly.
...
The lightning-bolt of Zeus
strikes the tallest mountain.

Aeschylus Agamemnon 450-70

The Chorus compare the women's lamentation over the dead to Menelaus' pain at the (temporary) loss of his wife. In so doing they question both the purpose of the war and the leaders who drove it on. In *Iliad* Book 9, Achilles offers a similar challenge to the ideological underpinnings of the Trojan adventure:

And why must the Greeks fight against the Trojans?
Why was it that Agamemnon led us all here?
Was it not for glorious Helen, Menelaus' wife?
Are the sons of Atreus alone among mortal men
in loving their wives?

Homer Iliad 9.337-41

Although focused on a mythic conflict, these examples from tragedy and epic anticipate (*mutatis mutandis*) the critics of recent wars fought by the US and its proxies, who point out the elite interests served by those campaigns. Even a cursory look at history explodes the claim that the US was fighting for justice, democracy, or self-determination when it overthrew (or tried to overthrow) the governments of Iran (1953), Guatemala (1954), Vietnam (1954-75), Cuba (1961-present), Zaire (1961), Dominican Republic (1965), Laos (1965-73), Cambodia (1970-5, then supporting the genocidal Pol Pot regime), Chile (1973), Angola (1975-90), Nicaragua (1980-90), Granada (1983), Panama (1989), Iraq (1990-present), Serbia (1998-2000) and Afghanistan (2001-2).

Like a Greek chorus, a small but vocal group keeps pointing to the underlying reasons behind these military actions, invasions, and *coups d'état*: control of oil and other natural resources; investment opportunities and 'reconstruction' contracts; the Pentagon system that funnels public money to private corporations (defence contractors, weapons manufacturers, 'strategic' research groups); corporate pressure for a cheap and docile labour force to assemble apparel,

105

computer chips, and manufactured goods; the expansion of agribusiness; and the accumulation of political, as well as economic, capital. 'No War for Oil' – the cry heard in protests at the US destruction of Iraq in 1990, after Iraq withdrew from Kuwait, and heard again today – represents a contemporary parallel to the Chorus' protest in *Agamemnon* against a war waged 'for another man's wife'.[17]

Democracy

Although postdating the myths on which Greek tragedy is based, aspects of Athenian democracy permeate the plays. We find references to democratic assemblies in Aeschylus' *Agamemnon* and *Suppliant Women*, Sophocles' *Ajax*, and Euripides' *Suppliant Women*, *Hecuba*, *Trojan Women*, and *Iphigenia in Aulis*. Jury trials modelled on democratic courts appear in Aeschylus' *Eumenides* and Euripides' *Orestes*, and allusions to fifth-century Athenian legal procedures run through many other tragedies. In spite of the 'royal' nature of Greek myth, tragedy remains remarkably grounded in radical Athenian democracy, a subject that scholars have explored in detail.[18]

More interesting for our purposes are the criticisms of democracy that surface in Greek tragedy. Although occasionally focussing on the idea that 'the many' are incapable of ruling, more often they attack politicians and public speakers who manipulate crowds in their own interest. In *Hecuba*, for example, the army is divided on whether or not to honour Achilles' ghost by sacrificing Polyxena at his tomb:

> the two sons of Theseus,
> offspring of Athens, made two speeches
> but of one mind and rhetoric. They argued that the army
> *should* crown Achilles' tomb with [Polyxena's] fresh blood.
> …
> The debate blazed zealously, equal on both sides,
> until Odysseus – that logic-chopping, mind-dazzling,
> honey-tongued crowd-pleaser – spoke.[19]
> He persuaded the assembled troops not to reject
> what the greatest of Greek warriors [Achilles] wanted
> just to keep from cutting the throat of a slave:
> 'Let none of those who fell at Troy, who stand

106

now in Persephone's realm, say that we
sailed off from the plains of Troy
without honouring those Greeks who died
on behalf of other Greeks.'

Euripides Hecuba 122-40

Persuaded by Odysseus, the Greeks vote to perpetrate one more horror at Troy. By introducing two *Athenians* who speak for Polyxena's death, Euripides brings the issue home to his audience.[20] Following their lead, Odysseus resembles an Athenian demagogue who flatters the crowd, disguising barbarism under the cloak of patriotic loyalty. As an embodiment of sophistic rhetoric, Odysseus also appears in *Trojan Women* (noted above) and *Philoctetes* (see Chapter 3), manifesting – in a mythical context – the violent potential of public 'debate'.

In similar fashion, we hear of a clever talker at the trial in Euripides' *Orestes*. The Messenger describes this character as the personification of meretricious speech and the dangers it poses for democracy:

Then there stood up
a man with no rein on his tongue, full of himself,
an Argive but not an Argive – just a bought mouth –
trusting in bluster and mindless speechifying,
but credible to the citizens, winding them in a net
of evil words.
...
This evil man prevailed, whipping up the mob
with his tongue, urging them to kill you and your sister.

Euripides Orestes 902-6, 944-5

We might view this fifth-century 'tongue-for-hire' as the ancient antecedent of the modern politician or spokesperson, paid by powerful interests to do their bidding while hiding behind the image of serving the public good.

We meet a most forthright challenge to democratic ideology in the unsympathetic but perceptive Theban Herald of Euripides' *Suppliant Women*:

[You trust] the man who fools the city with flattering words,
moving the rabble this way and that for his own profit.
At first he delights, promising great things,
but in the end he does damage, then hides his misdeeds
behind new slander, escaping the arm of justice.
And how can common people, who don't reason well,
know how to keep their city on course?
It takes time to learn how to do that – it doesn't come
in a flash. And what of the poor man, the farmer?
Even if he's not stupid, he can't look after
the common good, worn down as he is by hard work.

Euripides Suppliant Women 412-22

We recognize much here from our own political reality: lying speech, manipulation, criminality, the power of special interests, the lack of oversight, human stupidity and exhaustion, an overworked population with no time for self-government. Behind the Theban's aristocratic prejudice, we also catch a glimpse of Plato's later attack on democracy and its leaders. In the *Gorgias*, for example, Socrates compares the demagogue to a pastry chef offering the citizens cookies, when they really need medicine to restore the body politic to health. To bring the analogy into the modern world, the current-day politician owes his success not simply to the sweet tooth of his audience, but also to the financial backing of the butter, flour, and sugar tycoons who insist they do more for public health than doctors.

Education, indoctrination, identity

As we have seen, Greek tragedy offers a complex view of human beings, exposed to powerful influences of fear and pity, acting as both free agents and victims of fate, facing a life of contingency and mutability that may appear bleak but remains preferable to the sunless world of the dead. On top of these daunting paradoxes, tragic characters – and the fifth-century Athenians they reflect – find their domestic and political communities torn by violent and destructive forces. Would we be right to conclude that Greek tragedy views 'human nature' as inherently self-interested, self-divided, and self-destructive?

4. Tragedy and Ideology

We might hazard a short answer by pointing to the intrinsic nature of theatrical performance, which always holds out the hope for change. This hope arises from the fact that what occurs onstage in Greek tragedy depends on the presence of a non-fictional audience separate from the enacted story. Why would the Greeks or anyone else bother with this activity unless some possibility for pleasure, recognition, insight, or transformation remained open to those who witnessed it? Confronting the prospect that events might unfold pointlessly and at random, the Chorus of *Oedipus Tyrannus* famously ask, 'Then why is it necessary for us to dance?' (S. *OT* 896). As their question suggests, the narrative thrust of Greek tragedy already depends on the assumption that theatrical performance matters, that it has something meaningful to say to its audience.

Granted this possibility, let us consider how tragedy represents the education and indoctrination *into* Athenian ideology – that is, the concerted effort to influence and exploit whatever Athenian society assumed 'human nature' to be. As noted earlier, Sophocles' *Philoctetes* focuses on the education of Neoptolemus, who proves capable of resisting the worldview and orders of his commander Odysseus. Reflecting fifth-century anthropology, Neoptolemus demonstrates the human capacity to select among various influences, to develop a 'social compact', and to grow into virtue by rejecting simple obedience to military command.[21] The opposition to tyrannical power by the Choruses in Aeschylus' *Prometheus Bound*, *Suppliant Women*, *Agamemnon*, and *Libation Bearers*, and the courageous resistance of figures like Teucer in Sophocles' *Ajax* and the title characters in *Antigone* and *Electra*, dramatize the power of humans to act on their own beliefs, to resist enforced conformity, and to accept the consequences of their actions.

But what of the actual operations of indoctrination and propaganda? Some critics find them everywhere in Greek tragedy: in the Aristotelian form of the plays; in the idea of emotional and intellectual catharsis; in plots based on war, patriarchy, and the restoration of civil order; in the very notion of a tragic hero drawn from royalty; in the fact that the plays were produced at city-sponsored festivals, and were the work of male playwrights and male performers in a male-dominated society. On this view, Greek tragedy offers only negative paradigms for a modern audience, because the plays so

109

clearly reinforce the reigning ideology of the society that produced them.

Let us focus on a single instance where the process of ideology formation and indoctrination is explored: the funeral oration of Adrastos over the recovered bodies in Euripides' *Suppliant Women*. We learn earlier in the play that these dead heroes rejected the will of the gods, preferring an unholy war to a peaceful solution of their grievances. The Seven against Thebes have brought disaster on themselves and their community, and yet in the funeral oration Adrastos rewrites their history, turning them into paragons of virtue. The resonances extend to Athens, for Euripides models Adrastos' speech on the funeral orations delivered annually at the public burial of the Athenian war-dead, an event roughly equivalent to the President's speech at Arlington National Cemetery on Veterans' Day, or to similar patriotic occasions in other countries.

Two details emerge with particular force in Euripides' treatment. First, Theseus asks Adrastos to speak for the benefit of 'the young sons of these citizens' (Eur. *Su*. 843), referring to the Athenians in the audience.[22] That is, the occasion emphasizes tradition in its literal sense, the passing down of information to educate the young. Secondly, Adrastos ends his panegyric with a direct appeal to the importance and impact of such ideological training:

> Courage
> can be taught, for even a baby is taught
> by hearing and repeating what he cannot understand.
> Whoever learns lessons like that holds them close
> and keeps them till old age. So, teach your children well.
>   Euripides *Suppliant Women* 913-17

We find an echo of this indoctrinating view of education from the Sophist Protagoras as represented by Plato:

> Just as writing teachers trace letters with the stylus for children who are not yet good at writing, then give them the tablet and make them write following the outline of the letters, so also the city traces laws, the discoveries of good lawgivers long ago,

then makes people rule and be ruled following these, and who-
ever goes outside these it punishes.[23]

In this passage, Protagoras accepts indoctrination as normal, appropriate, and even necessary for social order. But as we have seen, far
from replicating such indoctrination, Greek tragedy provides distance and perspective on its processes, constituting a form of intellectual and emotional 'self-defence'. By dramatizing the many
contradictions between official and unofficial accounts, *Suppliant
Women* encourages the theatre audience not to follow rules but to
think critically about them.

As if influenced by Adrastos' 'profiles in courage', the young sons
of the dead warriors (the onstage audience of the speech) vow to
return to Thebes and exact vengeance for their fathers' deaths.
Nourished on military heroism, the young orphans will realize their
violent potential and guarantee that the cycle of killing continues, the
predictable outcome of their upbringing. The original audience was left
to reflect on their own ideological practices, especially when they
gathered to hear the annual funeral oration in praise of real Athenians who fell in battle. Perhaps they approached that civic occasion
more critically after Euripides' *Suppliant Women* than before it.

Indoctrination (as noted in the Introduction) has much to do with
identity, the markers we use to distinguish ourselves according to
gender, race, colour, class, sexual orientation, marital status, profession, political affiliation, and so on. When 'identity politics' surfaces
in Greek tragedy, it generally involves the audience in the question
of *Athenian* identity. Who are we? Who's in, who's out? Does who we
are relate to what we're doing? The character of Ion in Euripides'
eponymous play is instructive here, a young temple slave at Delphi
who turns out to be an Athenian prince. On learning that he can
aspire to Athenian rule, Ion resists leaving his idyllic world at
Apollo's shrine. Rather than rejoice at his reversal of fortune, Ion
fears the xenophobia he associates with Athens:

> Listen, father, to what's been on my mind.
> They say that Athenians are famous as earth's
> children, all native and no outsiders.[24]
> I'd come in with two afflictions –

111

as a bastard, and as son of a foreign-born king.

Euripides Ion 588-92

Instead of a safe harbour in Athens, Ion anticipates rejection and hardship due to his illegitimacy and his non-native status.

Ion also ponders the maelstrom of fifth-century Athenian politics:

> If I avoided power, I'd be nothing, a nobody.
> But if I joined the political fray
> and tried to *be* someone, the powerless
> would hate me. Achievement brings grief.
> On the other hand, capable men who wisely
> keep quiet and avoid political life
> would take me for a fool for speaking out
> in a city filled with fear.
> And if I succeeded, those active in Athens' interest
> might use the vote to shut me out.
> That's how these things tend to go, father.
> Men with power and privilege in the city
> are primed to fight their rivals.

Euripides Ion 594-606

The young man recognizes the paradoxical nature of Athenian political participation, damned if you do (subject to envy, contempt and ostracism), and damned if you don't (doomed to a life without influence).

Ion begs his father to let him ignore his good luck and remain happily where he is:

> Please listen, father. What I had here was good –
> quiet time, the most precious thing for humans,
> and cares I could master. No one shoves me
> out of the way here, or pushes me around. How hard
> it would be to deal with bullies, day after day.
> …
> I'm better off where I am, father.
> Let me live right here. The gift is the same,
> whether one delights in great things or small.

Euripides Ion 633-7, 645-7

With precocious understanding, Ion expresses no desire to be 'educated' out of his peaceful life in Delphi and into the dog-eat-dog world of contemporary Athens.

Of course, the audience knows that, far from representing an illegitimate foreign usurper, Ion is the son of the Athenian Queen Creusa and the god Apollo. As such, he represents the mythical root of the Ionian race, a line that includes Athenians and their traditional allies near the coast of Asia Minor, the backbone of the later Athenian empire. That the founder of an imperial race presciently criticizes what it will become suggests how Greek tragedy can look beyond ideology, encouraging the audience to question patriotic complacency. Reaching ahead of itself in its treatment of the city's founding myth, *Ion* exemplifies the rich interplay of past and future in Greek tragedy, the subject of the next chapter, 'Tragedy and Time'.

Political form

We noted above that some critics find tragic form intrinsically conservative, a dramatic structure built on tradition, hierarchy, programmed response and the inevitability of fate, with the implicit message that the human condition is pre-ordained, ahistorical, and not subject to meaningful change. Is tragedy a rule-bound system whose conventional structure can only support the status quo? Let us try to answer that question by looking more closely at the dissonance inherent in tragic form.

The presence of the Chorus in tragedy raises an obstacle to the seductions of character and character-driven plot, variations of which still dominate popular theatre today. The Chorus' relative freedom from the constraints of plot allows them to comment on the action and challenge its direction. As noted above, the Chorus introduce a spatial and temporal reach far beyond that required to 'tell the story'. Their evocation of natural forces, mythic events, and personified deities opens the world of tragedy to realms beyond ideological time-serving. The inclusive sweep of choral lyric – from folk memory and ritual to the most experimental 'new' music – hardly represents rote conventionalism. The variation in placement, tempo, length and metre of choral lyric suggests its inherent flexibility and resistance to a single interpretive or ideological function.

113

Like the Chorus, tragedy's larger-than-life characters do not operate by luring the audience into an intimacy that dulls their critical faculties. The front-footed acting style required to play mythic heroes and their associates in a large outdoor theatre drew the audience into the issues of the drama, and not primarily into the psychic space of its characters. Of course, tragedy summons up great passions, and audience sympathy (often a shifting phenomenon) plays a crucial role in the work of the plays. However, the *pathos* of tragic characters rarely represents suffering for its own sake. The pain and death in tragedy ask us to think about causes, and to consider the human resources needed to endure what frequently seems ruthless or undeserved.

In *Agamemnon*, the death of the returning hero raises a host of questions about what caused it – the role played by foreign war, by class and power, by familial relations, by the different paths open to men and women, by the past's influence on the present, by divine violence and retribution, by social, political, and moral beliefs. As discussed in Chapter 3, plays such as *Agamemnon* and *Oedipus Tyrannus* confront the nature of causality and the intricate web of agency and fate. Bertolt Brecht, however, compares an 'Aristotelian drama' like *Oedipus Tyrannus* to a burlesque show, where the inevitabilities of plot constitute a call for the hero to 'take it off!' like an erotic dancer urged by the crowd to reveal all.[25]

But Brecht fails to mention that Sophocles' play continues for a quarter of its length *after* Oedipus 'exposes' himself. What happens then, and why? Is Oedipus just one more naked body with nothing else to reveal? Is tragic fate so ideologically bound that it simply sets up another 'take-it-off' session? Oedipus' public revelations crack open a set of pre-existing assumptions, allowing an incestuous patricide to embrace his polluted children in the full knowledge of who he is and what he has done. The long denouement of *Oedipus Tyrannus* turns the 'striptease' into something very different, shifting from the revelations of the past to the uncharted future, which the blind protagonist has yet to live. As David Halliburton puts it, 'Oedipus knows the worst, but he does not yet know everything'.[26] We will say more about tragedy's opening to the future in the last chapter.

Finally, let us consider the ideology of form manifest in the Messenger speech. Joining descriptive narrative with horrific violence, these aria-like set speeches deliver some of the most intensely dramatic moments in tragedy. Because the interest lies in the message and not the messenger, the audience become essential co-creators of the event. As in a radio play, the spoken word releases the power of the imagination to evoke tragic acts in unseen places – within the palace (*Women of Trachis, Oedipus Tyrannus, Alcestis, Heracles*), on Mount Cithairon (*Bacchae*), at Apollo's sanctuary in Delphi (*Andromache*, Sophocles' *Electra*), at sea in the Aegean (*Agamemnon, Helen*), on the battlefield (*Seven Against Thebes, Phoenissae, Children of Heracles, Suppliant Women*), or in far-off Athens (*Persians*). Almost all Messenger speeches contain quoted dialogue, giving their recitation the feeling of a theatrical reenactment. Here Greek tragedy looks back to the traditions of oral poetry, where bards or rhapsodes narrated epic poems and played all the speaking characters as well.

Such non-spectacular means to open the mind's eye deserve our attention, inundated as we are with visual images that deaden the imagination and kill thought. To be sure, the right picture in the right context can disturb our view of the world and change our perspective on it. But, increasingly, visual images work like advertising, delivering a pre-digested message, whether on the network news or in the latest action film (both frequently produced by the same corporation – Time-Warner, Disney, Fox, Murdoch).[27] Given our contemporary aesthetic based on visual overkill, the fact that a tragic Messenger asks the audience to listen and conjure a world out of the spoken word represents a form of artistic resistance.

Reflecting the violent *pathos* of the events they describe, tragic Messengers frequently adopt a Homeric-like precision regarding physical details, from Oedipus stabbing his eyes with Jocasta's brooches to the Theban women ripping apart Pentheus and playing catch with his flesh. But unlike the visual excesses of Hollywood, which substitute for narrative content, a tragic Messenger speech invariably connects physical *pathos* to dramatic *peripeteia*. Horrible things happen within the context of a turn of the plot or reversal of fortune, which carries its own ideological critique. In *Oedipus Tyrannus*, the Messenger describes events in the palace, when Oedipus sees his mother-wife for the first time, hanging from a noose. He cuts Jocasta down and uses the brooches that fastened her dress to

115

obliterate the sight forever. In the *Bacchae*, the Messenger describes Pentheus sitting atop a pine tree spying on the Bacchic mysteries, until the women literally uproot his point-of-view and turn him from voyeur to victim. Reversals like these force the audience to confront the violent mutability of the world, the tragic pathos of *peripeteia*.

Even Messenger speeches announcing ostensible triumphs stir up strong counter-currents. The Herald in *Agamemnon* brings news of the Greek victory at Troy, but he also tells of the storm that destroyed the fleet as it sailed for home, 'the gods' anger' against the Greeks (A. *Ag.* 634-5). In Euripides' *Electra*, the Messenger's account of Orestes' victory over Aegisthus (*El.* 803-58) leaves us with a sense of moral repugnance. The gruesome assassination takes place at a rural sacrifice, overseen by a hospitable Aegisthus, who is axed in the back by Orestes. The twisted hero then brings the corpse to the farmer's cottage, where Electra abuses and reviles the body. In these examples, the triumph conveyed in a Messenger speech proves as transitory as the Messenger's appearance itself.

Consider the ideological crosscurrents that flow through the Messenger speech in Euripides' *Ion*. From a certain perspective, the Messenger reports a double triumph. Instructed by Xuthus, Ion erects a magnificent tent in which to celebrate his coming-of-age and 'rebirth' as an Athenian. In the course of the festivities, Creusa's old servant, disguised as a wine steward, poisons the cup meant for Ion to keep him from usurping Athenian rule. However, an ill-omened word causes the toast to be poured on the ground, where a flock of doves miraculously descends and one falls victim to the poison. Saved in the nick of time, Ion forces the wine-steward/servant to reveal that Creusa plotted his death, and he vows to kill her. But this double triumph – son found, son saved from death – is narrated by a servant of Creusa. From *his* perspective, the story is an unmitigated disaster, involving the salvation of a malicious interloper who now plans to kill the long-suffering Queen.

Besides its twists of plot and perspective, the Messenger speech features a description of the tent where Ion's transformation from innocent adolescent to vengeful adult takes place. Xuthus has Ion erect a pavilion large enough to house all of Delphi, whom he has invited to celebrate Ion's 'birthday'. The giant structure 'measures out to an enclosed area of 10,000 square feet,/ as the experts would say' (*Ion* 1138-9). Besides its grandeur and formal perfection, the Messenger emphasizes that the cambered poles, when covered, block out the sun (1132-6). This detail recalls the other sunless space in the play, the cave on the slope of the Athenian acropolis where Creusa, raped by Apollo, gave birth to Ion and later abandoned him.

The tent at Delphi bears an even closer link to Ion's native city. The frame supports a covering of tapestries from the Delphic treasury, gifts of Heracles (an extremely popular figure in Athens) when he conquered the Amazons. The Messenger describes the scenes depicted there, evoking an artistic counterworld to the sun-drenched sanctuary of Apollo, the setting of the play mirrored in the open-air theatre of Dionysus. The interior world 'created' by the Messenger has a roof covering that shows the heavens as if in a planetarium, with the dawn, sunset, moon, and constellations of the night sky. The Messenger singles out the Hyades, a group of stars associated with the daughters of the mythical Athenian king Erechtheus, who sacrificed them to save the city (mentioned earlier in the play at 277-82). On the sides of the tent, tapestries 'from barbarian lands' (1159) show a naval battle against the Greeks, probably the famous engagement at Salamis. Other scenes of conflict include images of the Centaurs, well known to Athenians from vase-paintings and from metopes carved on the Athenian Parthenon.

At the entrance of the tent, Ion places a statue of the snake-man Kekrops, grandfather of Erechtheus and symbol of Athenian autochthony. Kekrops stands with his daughters, whose suicidal leap off the Athenian acropolis is referred to several times in the play (21-6, 265-74). Pointedly, this gift to Apollo's sanctuary was 'the offering of some Athenian' (1164-5), suggesting that Ion has chosen an icon of Athens to mark the doorway through which he will leave Delphi for his new home.

This artificial world depicts cosmic order in the heavens, human conflict on the sides, and Athenian origin myths at the point of departure. It is in this context that Ion comes of age. His pristine world of service at Delphi gives way to a murder plot planned by Athenians, which in turn opens the floodgates of his own violence. Reflecting the ecphrastic iconography of the tent, Ion is caught between the animal instincts of the Centaurs or Kekrops and the lofty purity of the heavens woven into the overhead canopy. The nature of Ion's education is neither simple nor celebratory, and the fact that he leaves the tent crazed for blood points to a problematic future in Athens. This 'brave new world' Ion finds his voice when he returns to the stage, urging his cohorts to drag Creusa from Apollo's altar: 'Grab her! To the cliffs of Parnassos!/ There, hurl her like a discus over the edge./ Let the rocks comb out her lovely long hair' (1266-8).

In spite of these twists of plot and emotion, the play ends happily, with Ion and his mother reunited under the light of a beneficent Apollo, who shines over all. But the disturbing transformation described by the Messenger, and the Athenian iconography within which it occurs, point to the unsettling connection between violence in the blood and violence in the *polis*. When the adult Ion assumes his true place as a noble Athenian and founder of the Ionian race, we cannot forget his earlier judgement on the city that now claims him: petty, violent, politically divided, xenophobic, a place of deadly instincts and dangerous power.

Ion offered Athens a strange view of itself, foreign and native, divine and brutal, mythic and contemporary. The future of the city that produced the play constituted a *krisis* for its audience. And no simple notion of reinforced ideology could answer their troubling experience in the theatre. Recapturing the radical potential of Greek tragedy demands that we find our own way to recreate such disturbing effects. As I have argued in this chapter, one essential way to do so involves honouring the form of Greek tragedy and its capacity to resist ideological truisms that cover up deeply intractable problems.

5

Tragedy and Time

Time (*chronos*) purifies all things
as it grows old with them.
                    Aeschylus *Eumenides* 286

Time (*chronos*) uncovers all things and
brings them to light.
                    Sophocles fr. 918

Time (*chronos*) – the most variegated
lesson.
                    Euripides *Bellerophon* fr. 291.3

Ephemeral creatures, ephemeral art

As noted in the Introduction, several Greek terms for 'human beings' stress our temporal limits, notably *ephêmeroi*, 'beings of the day' (from *hêmera*, 'day'), and *thnêtoi*, 'those who die', as opposed to *athanatoi*, the immortal gods. The strong Greek emphasis on life as diurnal, temporary, and terminal feeds naturally into the theatre, the most ephemeral of the arts.

Live theatre vanishes as it happens, although subsequent performances may aim to recreate what has passed. Sharing in this transitory nature, the *mimêsis* of Greek tragedy (discussed in the Introduction) reflects the human reality that propels it into being. Like all theatrical performance, tragedy validates Yeats' paradox that 'things reveal themselves passing away'.[1] Frequently, tragedy refers directly to this passing, as in Sophocles' 'Ode to Man': 'Never without resources does man/ meet the future. But from death alone/ he finds no means of flight' (*Ant.* 360-2). Indeed, the Greek stage evoked enough killings and featured enough corpses to make death seem like

119

its natural focus. What director Antoine Vitez says of the theatre applies with special force to Greek tragedy: 'To do theater is to grow intoxicated with the ephemeral. To become inebriated with the passage of time. To get drunk on death.'[2] Living out its *moira*, tragic performance exposes – as it succumbs to – the limits of time.

If theatre is a series of vanishing acts, we should remember that something must be there first in order to disappear. For all its fugitive qualities, dramatic performance constitutes a remarkably concrete and material undertaking. For an ancient production of tragedy, we know that text, actors, director, costumes, masks, props, chorus members, musicians and stage equipment came together in the same space and time. Each of these elements had its own prior history, and a successful production depended on gathering, concentrating, and perfecting those various pasts in order to present them before the audience. In *The Empty Space*, Peter Brook underlines the aptness of the French word for rehearsal, *répétition*: 'Week after week, day after day, hour after hour, practice makes perfect. It is a drudge, a grind, a discipline; it is a dull action that leads to a good result.'[3] In a rehearsed production (as tragedy certainly was), a highly charged past takes the stage and asks for our attention; what we attend to is anything but the moment-to-moment evanescence of the spontaneous.

In *Art as Experience*, John Dewey distinguishes the art 'product' (frequently aestheticized, commercialized, or both) from the 'work of art', referring to the processes by which art comes into being and through which it affects others. For Dewey, the expressiveness of art involves the interaction of the artist's impulses, ideas, emotions and imagination with the demands of a given medium and its materials. The work of art is a manifestation of this mutually transformative process and cannot sensibly be divorced from it. Nor can we view it as independent from the audience whose experience it affects: 'The *work* of art ... takes place when a human being cooperates with the product so that the outcome is an experience that is enjoyed because of its liberating and ordered properties.'[4] A transitory form like the theatre offers up its accumulated pasts to the audience's experience in the present, and in the future. By exploring temporal qualities intrinsic to Greek tragedy, we may awaken a deeper sense of how performance and time might work together now.

5. Tragedy and Time

Building blocks of time

We have trouble understanding time without using spatial metaphors. On the job, we pile up sick leave or vacation time. We speak of time as having length and different points, we imagine the past as lying behind us and the future as stretching out ahead. Some think of time as a vast ocean, or as a river flowing through space, coming and going and never standing still. We talk of the hereafter, not the 'nowafter' or 'thenafter'. Reflecting day-to-day dependence on the land and the natural world, the ancient Greeks considered time and space as inseparable. They marked seasons by the stars, months by the moon, days and nights by the sun, as the Watchman indicates when recalling his yearlong vigil in *Agamemnon*:

> I know all about the gathering stars,
> which bring us summer and which winter,
> when they rise and set, those
> bright powers gleaming in the sky ...
> Aeschylus *Agamemnon* 4-7

On a smaller scale, the Greeks never lost their connection between time and real events.[5] In the lawcourts, for example, Athenians used the traditional Mediterranean *klepsydra*, or 'water-stealer', which measured out equal allotments of time for plaintiffs and defendants to speak to the jury. This device signalled the passage of time via a given volume of water that flowed out of the container; a speaker spoke until the water ran out, the vacated space marking his elapsed 'space' of time. Abstract temporal notions – time as number, for example, as in our digital watches or rocket 'countdowns' – played little role in the ancient world.

In *Timaeus* Plato famously describes time as the 'moving image of eternity'. Because the eternal forms never change, they must lie 'outside' time to remain 'timeless'. Aristotle associates time directly with motion and physical change in celestial objects, natural phenomena, animals, and humans. Without this change, we would have no awareness of, or curiosity about, time.[6] In his *Critique of Pure Reason*, Kant applies Aristotle's insight to a more immediate experience of change, that of human consciousness itself. For Kant, time is

121

(at minimum) an *a priori* perception of internal mental change, reflecting our intermittent but ongoing awareness of being aware, of thinking, of having experiences at all.[7]

We may perceive time as internal or external change or motion, but Greek tragedy explores the larger shape of those movements, incorporating basic Greek concepts of time in the process. In *Children of Heracles*, for example, the Chorus contemplate the miraculous rejuvenation of Iolaus, Heracles' ancient comrade, transformed into a youthful and victorious battle hero:

> For all-completing fate [*Moira*] and the span
> of one's life [*Aiôn*], child of time [*Chronou*],
> bring many things to pass.
>> Euripides *Children of Heracles* 898-900

'All-completing fate' we discussed in Chapter 3; let us consider the other two temporal terms in this passage, *chronos* and *aiôn*.

Chronos is time understood as an enduring continuum, but its child *aiôn* represents an individual life, a specific lifespan, or an epoch within time's wider extension. In the opening chorus of Aeschylus' *Agamemnon*, Calchas prophesies the future of the Greek expedition to Troy: 'In time [*chronôi*] you will seize Priam's city ...' (*Ag.* 126). On the verge of war, Calchas looks ahead a decade, just as the Chorus look back 'Ten years!' (*Ag.* 40) on the events that preceded the Trojan campaign. *Chronos* seems to stretch out in both directions, but its 'offspring' *aiôn* is born to die, as Iphigenia discovers: 'Her prayers and cries of "Father",/ her virgin's span of life [*aiôna*] meant nothing/ to the warloving leaders ...' (*Ag.* 228-30). Iphigenia's sacrifice enables the Greek fleet to sail, but it leads to many more deaths, culminating in the sack of Troy, the outcome of *chronos* to which Calchas refers in his prophecy. As the trilogy makes brutally clear, however, *chronos* extends beyond Troy, bringing to an end the lifespan of others closer to home.

We can find passages where *chronos* refers to different aspects of time, but generally it suggests this broad sweep, as when Philoctetes describes his solitary life on Lesbos: 'So time [*chronos*] kept moving on for me, year after year [*dia chronou*]' (S. *Ph.* 285). The wounded hero reflects on his own survival and wishes that his time were up:

'O hated span of life [*aiôn*], why, why do you keep me above, looking/ on the light, and not send me down to Hades?' (*Ph.* 1348-9). Tragic characters think of time as an agent, acting on them by offering the temporal space in which they suffer, prosper, or die.

Touching a motif discussed in Chapter 2, the Chorus of Euripides' *Suppliant Women* have lost their sons and wish their lives had gone otherwise:

> Would that old father Time (*Chronos*)
> had made me unmarried still and always,
> even to this very day.
> Why did I need children?
>> Euripides *Suppliant Women* 786-9

In a similar vein, Iphis arrives to bury his son only to find himself witnessing the suicide of his daughter Evadne. Inconsolable, Iphis wishes for two lives so that he could live the second based on what he'd learned from the first:

> Oh god! Why isn't it possible for mortals
> to be young and old once and then once again?
> When something at home doesn't go well, we can
> make it right later using what we've learned.
> But this isn't possible with one lifespan [*aiôna*].
>> If only we could
> be young and old twice! Then, if we failed the first time,
> we could get it right in our second run at life.
>> Euripides *Suppliant Women* 1080-6

In that second life, Iphis would not have children because he had experienced the pain of their loss in this one.

As well as the sweep of *chronos* and the truncated span of *aiôn*, the Greeks understood time as having cyclical and punctual aspects. For the former, they used the term *hôra*, 'season', the root of English 'hour' and 'year'; for the latter, *kairos*, meaning 'appropriate time', 'right moment'. In *Oedipus Tyrannus*, the Chorus wonder what the Delphic oracle reported by Creon portends:

> Oh healer Apollo,
> we stand in awe of you –
> what will you bring to pass? Some new thing, or
> something returning with the revolving seasons [*hôrais*]?
>
> Sophocles Oedipus Tyrannus 154-7

The 'new thing' points to an instant of intervention, but the Chorus acknowledge that the god also works through the natural cycle of seasons. Approaching the truth of his birth, Oedipus summons the shepherd who gave him as an infant to the messenger from Corinth: 'It is high time [*kairos*] these things were found out' (*OT* 1050). The actual moment of discovery takes place in a scene that *reunites* the three parties originally on Cithaeron. That is, the 'new thing' comes to light as part of an earlier pattern,[8] anticipating Dewey's description of sudden visual recognition:

> When a flash of lightning illumines a dark landscape, there is a momentary recognition of objects. But the recognition is not itself a mere point in time. It is the focal culmination of long, slow processes of maturation. It is the manifestation of the continuity of an ordered temporal experience in a sudden discrete instant of climax.[9]

Oedipus' discovery comes out of the past and is certainly climactic. However, as discussed in Chapter 4, it does not mark the end of the play, which from this point on opens onto a future that is unseen, in more ways than one.

In Euripides' *Alcestis*, the Chorus proclaim that the heroine's glory will live on 'cyclically':

> The poets will sing your praises
> ...
> whenever in Sparta the circling month [*hôra mênos*]
> of Carneios [ca. August] comes around,
> and the full moon sits on high all night long;
> so too in Athens ...
>
> Euripides Alcestis 445-52

Alcestis' singular act of dying for her husband will last forever by returning annually, much like a Christian saint's day, when martyrdom and miracle come around each year and are celebrated in the liturgy. Such cyclical patterns regulated many aspects of Athenian life, including dramatic festivals like the City Dionysia, which arrived in the early spring, year after year.

In more heavily 'plotted' tragedies, however, *kairos* holds far greater importance than *hôra*, because the action must happen at the right moment to prove effective. Orestes in Sophocles' *Electra* asks his sister not to recount the horrors she has suffered, for they will lose 'the proper moment of time' (*kairon chronou* 1293) to act on their revenge. The Tutor echoes Orestes' advice – 'now [*nun*] is the time [*kairos*] to act' – and he repeats the word 'now' three times in two lines (S. *El.* 1368-9). The moment has come, and delay means failure.

We find a prospective sense of *kairos* in *Ion*, where Xuthus decides to wait for 'the right moment in time' (*kairon chronôi*) before asking Creusa to hand over the rule of Athens to Ion (Eur. *Ion* 659). In *Prometheus Bound*, the Chorus inquire about the future of Zeus' rule, prompting Prometheus to say 'It is not the right time [*kairos*] to talk about this' (A. *PV* 522-3). And in *Helen*, the heroine recognizes that Menelaus' shipwreck, which seemed disastrous, is perfectly timed for their escape: 'Saved at the right time [*kairon*], destroyed at the wrong [*akaira*]' (Eur. *Hel.* 1081). *Kairos* is about timing – the propitious conjunction of agent, opportunity, means, and moment – a central concern of Greek tragedy.[10]

Tragic modalities of time

What Dewey says about the complexity of human temporal response applies with special force to our earliest drama:

> Time ceases to be either the endless and uniform flow or the succession of instantaneous points which some philosophers have asserted it to be. It, too, is the organized and organizing medium of the rhythmic ebb and flow of expectant impulse, forward and retracted movement, resistance and suspense, ... [pointing to] fulfillment and consummation ... [which in turn] become the initial points of new processes of development.[11]

125

Let us look at some ways that the tragedians organize the 'rhythmic ebb and flow of expectant impulse', heightening the spectator's awareness of time as they gather the past towards the future.

A technique used in many genres to build dramatic pressure involves 'barrier time', a limit or deadline against which the action must play out.[12] In *Heracles*, the hero arrives in the nick of time to save his family from Lycus' butchery. Euripides' Medea has but one day to work her revenge, before her exile from Corinth takes effect (Eur. *Med.* 340-54). Calchas prophesies that Ajax will survive the shame of his madness only if he remains inside his tent for the duration of that single day (S. *Aj.* 749-57). In *Women of Trachis*, Tecmessa recalls that Heracles fixed an exact time of fifteen months for his return, having learned from the oracle at Dodona that he either would die then or survive to live the rest of his life free from pain (S. *Trach.* 164-74). The play takes place on that fateful day, with fatal consequences.

Such temporal constraints play a crucial role in Hollywood thrillers and action films, where the roller-coaster of suspense keeps the audience on the edge of their seats. Will the heroine find out that her husband is the killer before he poisons her? Will the secret agent track down the atomic bomb and dismantle it in time? Unlike its exploitation for suspense in popular movies, barrier time in Greek tragedy focuses attention on *how* events unfold, not on what will happen next. Hollywood's incessant push to the next car-chase, the next shoot-out, the next explosion, the next escape uses barrier time repetitively, minimising any depth of discovery in the process. This kind of 'temporal rush' has little to do with how tragedy works with time.

Rather than an orgasmatron of emotional suspense and release (precisely what Aristotle's catharsis is *not*), Greek tragedy explores the complexity of temporal experience within the highly compressed time of its performance.[13] The different modes of tragic expression have their own dominant sense of time. Compare, for example, the rapid exchange of single lines (and sometimes half-lines) called stichomythia ('speech by lines', also a Shakespearean device) with the slower rhythm and pace of a prologue or monologue. Paired speeches, usually agonistic and of roughly equal length, measure themselves against each other like law-court pleas or public debates.

Agamemnon responds to Clytemnestra's welcoming oration: 'Off-spring of Leda, guardian of my house,/ your speech was like my absence – / it went on far too long' (A. *Ag.* 914-16). Medea opens her assault on Jason with the rhetorical 'I will begin my speech from the beginning'. By way of rebuttal, Jason responds, 'It seems that I must show myself no mean speaker ...' (Eur. *Med.* 475, 522). By calling attention to the preceding or impending speech, a dramatic character changes the audience's temporal experience of what is being said, asking us to attend to the *fact* of the speech as well as to its content.[14]

In addition to speech and dialogue, tragedy uses choral lyric in various tempi determined by the poetic metre, the music, the text, and the choreography. Lifting the play beyond constraints of speech and character, the Chorus can accomplish something like a 'time out' from the plot. In the *parodos* and first stasimon of *Agamemnon*, for example, the Chorus make us feel that a great deal of time has passed between the arrival of the beacon (signalling Troy's fall nearly at the speed of light) and that of the Herald only 400 lines later. No one in the audience thinks the ships from Troy have arrived too quickly, because the intervening choral lyric – moving freely between past and present – has expanded our sense of passing time.[15]

In *Antigone*, the 'Ode to Man' follows the Guard's report that Polyneices' body has mysteriously been covered with earth. 'You will never see me coming here again', the Guard asserts on his exit, happy to have escaped Creon's wrath with his life (S. *Ant.* 329-31). The Chorus follow with an ode praising the achievements of humans, hymning their progress over time. The temporal sweep could not be greater, and the ode seems to have little to do with any immediate dramatic context. However, at its conclusion, the Guard unexpectedly returns with Antigone as his captive, effectively framing the Chorus' reflections on the larger human story with the harsh realities of this one. Here, the dramatic time of the plot impinges on the Chorus' narrative of temporal progress, subverting their celebration of human accomplishment.

An actor's monody combines solo movement and accompanied song, personalizing the experience of time while externalizing it physically. In Euripides' *Electra* (112-66), the protagonist sings as she carries water back from the spring, her monody evolving into a tortured reminiscence of past and present suffering. Creusa's lyric confession of her rape by Apollo in *Ion* (859-922) brings out the hidden shame that has shaped her past and has brought her to Delphi in search of a son. Antigone's wedding-and-funeral dirge with the Chorus in *Antigone* (806-82) reveals the underside of her morbidly resolute character, juxtaposing the non-burial of her brother with her own wedding to death. In these songs, the combination of music, text and movement allow for a freer evocation of time as experienced by an individual character.

A lyric 'dialogue' between character and Chorus joins the confrontation basic to rhetoric with the ensemble mode of choral performance. The combination can quicken the dramatic pulse, as in the Cassandra-Chorus lyric scene in *Agamemnon* (1072-177) or the *kommos* in *Choephori* (306-478). Alternatively, it can intensify and prolong a shared sense of grief, as in the funereal *kommos* between Adrastos and the Chorus in *Suppliant Women* (778-837). The variety of expressive modes in tragedy – prologue, monologue, dialogue, stichomythia, paired speeches, choral lyric, actor monody, lyric dialogue – indicates the genre's temporal flexibility. The different experiences of time can emerge, however, only if one honours the form that sustains them and ties them to the play's overall narrative.

Time as a force of nature

By virtue of its mythic context, tragedy's drive toward recognition and *peripeteia* ('dramatic reversal') operates on both a moment-to-moment *and* a macro-temporal level. Knowing the mythic background, audiences in the ancient theatre experienced tragedy through the filter of earlier versions of the story, some of them even parodied in the new treatment. By virtue of this double focus, the tragedians could avoid the incessant forgetting of past time that dramatic suspense demands. Moreover, as discussed in Chapter 1, ancient spectators watched tragic stories unfold against the permanent background of nature and the built environment of the Athenian *polis*, not in a darkened room where the only world that matters is onstage, or racing by at 24 frames per second on the screen. The multiple contexts of Greek tragedy encourage the expansion of dramatic time beyond the ticking clock that regulates much contemporary life and art. We can see this process exemplified in two contrasting works, Aeschylus' *Oresteia* and Euripides' *Electra*.

Aeschylus' trilogy moves forward and backward through time via the memories and expectations of the characters, the lyrical sweep of the Chorus, and the prophecies of Calchas, Cassandra, and Athena. In these recollections of the past and anticipations of the future, aspects of the natural world emerge to reconfigure the story, as noted above in the Watchman's prologue set against the stars. Let us focus on time in the trilogy as it connects to the natural forces of procreation, maturation, death, and regeneration, elements essential to the working of the *Oresteia*.

In the *parodos* ('entrance song') of *Agamemnon*, the Chorus invite us to see the human drama through parallels with the animal world. They liken Menelaus' loss of Helen to eagles who find their nest robbed of its young (*Ag.* 42-54). At Aulis eagles appear again, at first auspiciously, on the right side as omens good for war. However, they then swoop down on a pregnant hare, her womb swollen with young, and feast (*Ag.* 111-20). Whether as victims or predators, the eagles evoke the death of innocent offspring, a fact that angers Artemis, goddess of birth and wildlife. To balance the eagle omen at Aulis, she demands that Agamemnon sacrifice his own daughter Iphigenia (literally, 'strong in [or at] birth') in order for the Greek ships to sail to Troy. The empty nest and murdered young gather multiple associations through the trilogy, implicating in various ways Helen, Iphigenia, Artemis, Agamemnon, Clytemnestra, Cassandra (whose visions include the butchered children of Thyestes), Aegisthus, Orestes, Electra, and even the Furies.

In a variation on the theme of young animals, the Chorus sing of a lion cub torn away from its mother and raised as a pet (*Ag.* 717-36). Cradled in people's arms like a baby, the cub proves gentle with children and fawns playfully for food and attention. In the course of time (*chronistheis*), however, the lion manifests the true nature it 'received from its parents' (727-8), making it a born hunter who slaughters cattle and wreaks havoc in the house. An innate inheritance 'grows up' with the animal, eventually revealing the creature's basic instincts and proclivities. In the world of nature, time cannot be frozen, nor can it be viewed abstractly. Rather, it operates within the principles of growth and maturation, of fulfilment and revelation.

We see this process at work in Clytemnestra's description of the beacon that announces the fall of Troy (*Ag.* 281-316). Although the dominant metaphor suggests a relay race, with the fire 'passed on' at successive watchposts across the Aegean, Clytemnestra announces its arrival at Argos as follows: 'And then, it leapt down on the roof of the house of Atreus,/ a flame descended [lit. "not without ancestor"] from the fire at Troy' (310-11). The beacon brings news of victory, but it also carries with it the devastation inherited from its forebears at the sack of the city. The flames fatefully link past to present, Troy to Argos, the house of Priam to that of Atreus, a fatal union that comes to fruition in the murder of Agamemnon and Cassandra.

On his return, Agamemnon reports how the Greeks sacked Troy. In describing the trick of the wooden horse, he uses a complex image that draws together humans, animals, birth, bloodshed, and the stars:

> The beast of Argos ground the city to dust.
> Shield-bearing young of the wooden horse
> timed their birth to the setting Pleiades.
> A ravening lion leapt the tyrant's walls
> and lapped its fill of the blood of kings.
> > Aeschylus *Agamemnon* 824-8

Like the lion cub in the Chorus, over time the Greek army reveals its bloodthirsty nature, a monster born to kill, and yet its birth is aligned with the stars. The temporal interconnections between human action (leaving the horse to sack the city) and the natural world (the image of birth, the setting constellation) recall the interworkings of fate and agency discussed in Chapter 3.

In *Choephori*, Orestes hears of the nightmare that prompted his mother to send graveside offerings to placate Agamemnon's spirit (523-39). Clytemnestra dreamed she gave birth to a snake that sucked her blood when she nursed it. Orestes correctly interprets that he himself is the monster who was born to kill his mother: 'For I, having turned into a snake,/ will kill her, as this dream predicts' (*Cho.* 549-50). At the point of death, Clytemnestra also sees what Orestes has become, recognizing her own role as the mother who brought him to it: 'Ah, me! I gave birth to this snake and reared it' (*Cho.* 928).

Just as Orestes is the son of Agamemnon and Clytemnestra, so his parents are the products of their own genealogical past. 'Offspring of Atreus' the Chorus call Agamemnon (*Ag.* 784), and he addresses Clytemnestra as 'Offspring of Leda' (914), the mother of Helen as well as Clytemnestra. Time in the *Oresteia* constantly recuperates the past by emphasizing the human generation that brings us into the world of time to begin with. This process culminates with the transformation of the Furies in the final play into protectors of childbirth and marriage. At the outset, these 'daughters of night' (*Eum.* 321-2) appear monstrous, compared to gorgons, harpies, hunting dogs, serpents and blood-sucking vampires (34-59, etc). During the trial of Orestes their bestial masks and costumes remain, but the Furies gradually assume the attributes of law-court prosecutors. After their final conversion, they don the purple robes of Athenian metics, taking up permanent residence in the city of the audience, their potential for transformation realized through the workings of time.

Early in *Eumenides* (179-97), Apollo throws the Furies out of the *omphalos* at Delphi, the sacred 'navel' of the world. By the end of the play, however, Athena grants them a home in Athens, where these 'ancient virgins' (so called at 67-8) receive honours connected to marriage and childbirth. As the trilogy moves from the mythic past of the Trojan War to the future of Athens and its civic institutions (the Areopagos court, the Panathenaia), so the Furies grow from avengers of kindred bloodshed to guardians of wedded life and future offspring. In the *Oresteia*, time is embedded in the natural processes of procreation, maturation, and regeneration. Events may disrupt or derail those processes, but without them there is no real time in the trilogy, and no long-term future for its audience.

In contrast, Euripides' *Electra* seems to undermine the idea of a future worth considering, or a past that can be recovered. Married off to a poor farmer while remaining a virgin, Electra pretends to have borne a son, a ruse to lure her mother out to the countryside to perform the required birth ritual. In the cottage Clytemnestra meets her death at the hands of her own children, following Orestes' gruesome murder of Aegisthus at a sacrifice. Euripides tears from the myth the remnants of tragic nobility and divine sanction, leading some critics to posit a kind of temporal 'nihilism' that deracinates the present from the past.

Euripides challenges the basic assumptions of the story in various ways: the anti-heroic setting (rural farm, not royal palace); untraditional characterizations (a cowardly Orestes, a harridan Electra); theatrical parody (Electra mocks the signs used in Aeschylus' *Choephori* to prove Orestes' identity in the recognition scene); the doubting of mythic explanations by the Chorus (who find them incredible, albeit morally useful, at *El.* 737-46). In Euripides' version, even the gods question the gods. Appearing on high, the deified Castor disapproves of Apollo's oracle that encouraged the matricide. Similarly, Castor's revelation about Zeus – he sent a phantom Helen to Troy to cause a long war and depopulate the earth (1280-3) – makes the Olympian overlord particularly cruel and inhuman. Finally, Castor's blandishments that Orestes and Electra should look happily toward the future (1308-42) contrast so markedly with the human characters' reactions to the situation (blood-guilt, fear of exile and separation) that the god seems to have landed in the wrong play.

By contrasting the dramatic present with the mythic past and projected future, however, Euripides does not invalidate either past or future time. Rather, he exposes how they can be idealized, romanticized, manipulated, covered up, or lied about. Of course, an idealized past *can* capture the truth about innocent hopes that rise up before the realities of events destroy them. For example, the Chorus follow the farmer's folksy thoughts about food ('given a full stomach, there's no difference between rich and poor', 430-1) by evoking the heroic departure of the Greek ships for Troy:

> Oh famed ships, you long ago set sail for Troy,
> and on the pull of countless oars
> danced among the chorus of Nereids [sea nymphs].
> Ahead, the flute-loving dolphins gambolled,
> there where the prows rose and fell,
> ploughing through the dark blue crests.
>
> Euripides *Electra* 432-7

This choral 'gear-shift' leaves the mundane world of the Farmer for the heroic world of myth, exemplifying how lyric in tragedy can introject a radically different tone and sense of time. By the end of the chorus, however, the initial celebration has given way to violence, as the lyric moves towards the destruction at Troy and the impending murder of Clytemnestra (*El.* 476-86).

Scholars date the play between 420 and 410 BCE, opening up the possibility that the ode alludes to Athens' disastrous Sicilian expedition of 415-13. There, too, the fleet sailed off with high hopes for foreign conquest, only to suffer the worst Athenian disaster of the Peloponnesian War.[16] This historical event may help explain Castor's closing lines:

> We [Castor and his brother] two shall make haste to Sicily
> in order to save the ships that cross the sea ...
> ...
> Let no one choose to act unjustly,
> or to sail together with oath-breaking shipmates.
> Being a god, I give that advice to mortals.
>
> Euripides *Electra* 1347-8, 1354-6

Whatever the play's date, the pattern of the 'Trojan War' chorus mirrors the Athenians' experience during their war with Sparta. The fact that Zeus concocted the conflict at Troy to decimate the human race via a 'phantom' Helen (as we learn belatedly from Castor) may suggest a similar prospective relevance to the 'phantom' reasons for the Peloponnesian War, as noted in the discussion of *Helen* in Chapter 4. Although such conclusions remain hypothetical, we should note that the relationship of Euripides' *Electra* to his own world is comparable to that of Aeschylus' *Oresteia*, which moves from Argos and the past to Athens and its contemporary democracy.

Similarly, the temporal cycle of nature operates in Euripides' version as it does in Aeschylus', albeit in a humbler and less symbolic way. As noted above, Euripides sets the play before the rural cottage of a poor farmer, the erstwhile husband of Electra. Together they discuss the daily chores of gathering water, cleaning house, preparing food, and so on (*El.* 64-76, 402-25). The farmer talks of tilling the soil for spring planting (78-81), and of the hardships of poverty and the satisfactions of a full stomach (426-31). Later, the old Tutor of Orestes, who pastures sheep in the countryside, arrives at the cottage with fruits of the land – a lamb, cheese, wine – to feed Electra's guests, the incognito Orestes and Pylades. The place and processes of farm life ground the play, until their daily and seasonal rhythms get hijacked by the reunited siblings' drive for revenge. It is as if anachronistic aristocrats have invaded the Greek countryside, until the poor cottage suffers not from an empty larder but from an excess of corpses.

The temporal processes of childbirth, child-rearing, maturation and regeneration, so prominent in Aeschylus' trilogy, also occur in Euripides' *Electra*, although in a twisted and perverted fashion. The *fear* of offspring, discussed in Chapter 2, looms large when Aegisthus marries Electra off to the impoverished farmer to keep her from having noble sons. He fears that she otherwise might wed a powerful husband and bear him children who could avenge her (19-28, 34-44). On several occasions Electra bewails her sexless and childless state. She refuses the Chorus' invitation to attend the Argive festival of Hera, the goddess associated with marriage. Electra assails Aegisthus and Clytemnestra for their sexual congress, and she ridicules the children that result (62-6, 916-37, 1089-90).[17] As noted above, Electra even uses the stratagem of a non-existent newborn to lure her mother to her death.

After the murder of Clytemnestra, both Orestes and Electra are consumed with guilt at having killed the woman who gave them life. 'I am the guilty one', Electra insists, 'wretch that I am, I went like fire after my mother, who bore me as her daughter' (1182-5). Because of the matricide, brother and sister consider their future hopeless:

> *Orestes*: To what other city can I go?
> What host, what decent person
> would even look at me,
> a man who killed his mother?
> *Electra*: Ah me, me! Where can I go? to what dances,
> to what marriage? What husband would take me
> to his bridal bed?
>
> Euripides *Electra* 1194-200

Castor addresses these concerns, promising Electra a husband (Pylades, who will take her home to Phocis), and foretelling Orestes' acquittal in Athens and his founding of a new city. However, cut off from their natal and native past, neither sister nor brother is buoyed by the prospect.[18]

The prosperity that Castor promises seems hollow, undermined by the bloody corpses that remain after the gods, characters and Chorus depart. Euripides' *Electra* has time for many things, but not for a happy ending that requires we forget the brutality of events that have come before. Euripides offers a timely warning for those in the contemporary world who rush towards a 'better tomorrow', provided they can ignore the violence and inequality of the past on which their present and future may be built.

Archetypes and time

Tragedy frequently involves archetypal characters facing a transition in their biological or social development. In *Electra*, for example, we have the nubile Chorus of maidens, the still virgin protagonist, her ephebe-aged brother and his friend Pylades; the matronly but still fertile Clytemnestra; and the old Tutor, almost literally on his last legs. Like people everywhere, the ancient Greeks marked these stages of development with rites of passage at birth, puberty, marriage, maternity, paternity, and death. Fertility and birth rituals feature prominently in Electra, including Aegisthus' sacrifice to the nymphs (625-7, 1134-5), and Electra's invented newborn that requires Clytemnestra's ritual assistance. Weddings lie behind the Argive festival of Hera and the Chorus' visit to Electra; Clytemnestra recalls the false wedding-turned-sacrifice of her daughter Iphigenia (1020-3); and the play ends with the promise of a 'real' marriage for Electra and Pylades, fulfilling her belated transition from maiden to bride. As for Orestes, his bloodletting constitutes a perverted rite of passage from adolescence to adulthood, setting up the death ritual for his victims Aegisthus and Clytemnestra that Castor outlines near the end (1276-80).

Tragedy concentrates on key, transitional phases of life, experiences shared in different epochs and cultures. We meet a plethora of ephebic males in tragedy, inexperienced sexually or in battle: Orestes, Pylades, Hyllus (*Women of Trachis*), Haimon, Neoptolemus, Hippolytus, Ion, Pentheus, Menoeceus (*Phoenician Women*). Virginal, unmarried, or soon-to-be-wedded young women play important roles in their respective plays: the Danaids, Io, Antigone, Ismene, Electra, Chrysothemis, Iphigenia, Polyxena, Cassandra (in *Trojan Women)*, Hermione (in *Orestes*), and the Choruses of Euripides' *Ion*, *Electra*, and *Phoenician Women*. Old men, their lives apparently behind them, appear in *Agamemnon* (Chorus), *Oedipus Tyrannus* (the shepherd), *Oedipus at Colonus* (Oedipus), *Alcestis* (Pheres), *Andromache* (Peleus), *The Children of Heracles* (Iolaus, Chorus), *Heracles* (Amphitryon, Chorus), *Bacchae* (Teiresias, Cadmus), *Suppliant Women* (Iphis), *Orestes* (Tyndareus), and *Electra* and *Ion* (the old Tutors). Their female counterparts, often maternal or grandmotherly figures, take the stage in *Suppliant Women* (Chorus), *Alcestis* (Nurse), *Ion* (Pythia), and *Hecuba* and *Trojan Women* (Hecuba). Even immature children appear more frequently than one might imagine – Eurysakes in *Ajax*, Molossus in *Andromache*, Astyanax in *Trojan Women*, young children in *Oedipus Tyrannus*, *Alcestis*, *Medea*, *Hecuba*, *Heracles*, and *Children of Heracles*.

By acknowledging the biological and social phases through which humans pass, tragedy appeals to the common realities of birth and childhood, the transition from adolescence, the pressures and prospects of marriage and children, the decline of old age, the grief and closure of death. It does so implicitly, by framing the action as a conflict between parent and child (*Antigone*, *Choephori*, the two *Electras*, *Oedipus at Colonus*), between youth and maturity (*Medea*, *Alcestis*) or old age (*Persians*, *Suppliant Women*, *Bacchae*), between those with children and those without (Euripides' *Electra*, *Suppliant Women*, *Andromache*, *Ion*), and so on.[19] The genre's interest in cross-generational conflict means that we frequently find three generations onstage at the same time – in *Agamemnon*, *Oedipus at Colonus*, *Philoctetes* (at the end), *Andromache*, *Hecuba*, *Suppliant Women*, *Trojan Women*, *Children of Heracles*, *Heracles*, *Ion*, and *Orestes*. In other words, tragic conflict does not arise from personal idiosyncrasies (as it might today), nor does it exist solely within a family, between the sexes, or among different cities and political groups. It also grows out of differences in temporal perspective reflecting different stages of life, tapping archetypes at the core of human experience.

Time and the audience

To summarize, we have observed how tragedy avoids the incessant 'now and impending' drive basic to much contemporary theatre and dramatic entertainment.[20] Tragedy incorporates and demands a much broader temporal experience by virtue of its rootedness in myth, its links to the natural world, its different expressive modes (with their particular 'time signatures'), its acknowledgement of previous mimetic practice, and its representation of human transformation as archetypal stages rather than individual achievements. Tragedy captures the complex interplay of past, present, and future by drawing together various Greek aspects of time – extended (*chronos*), epochal (*aiôn*), interventionist (*kairos*), and cyclical (*hôra*) – all of which are given presence in the ephemeral art of the theatre.

Because a familiar myth usually frames the plot, tragedy has a past that it shares with the audience (at least the original fifth-century audience).[21] In most cases, modern drama must provide its own background, and part of the playwright's task involves filling in the context 'naturally' through dialogue, going 'forward into the past'. Of course, Greek tragedy does the same (usually in the prologue or the opening chorus [*parodos*]), but its manifestations of the 'non-present' can involve less predictable methods. Ghosts temporarily rise from the dead (Darius in *Persians*, Polydorus in *Hecuba*) to divulge the past and predict the future. Prophets reveal what has already happened as well as what is to come (Teiresias, Cassandra). Stage objects and properties evoke bygone days that animate the present (Agamemnon's tomb in *Choephori*, Hector's shield in *Trojan Women*, the birth tokens in *Ion*), or infect the future (Phaedra's letter in *Hippolytus*, Nessus' poison in *Women of Trachis*). The accumulation of corpses, a frequent feature of tragedy, represents the past as dead but materially present, provoking the living to recount events that brought the bodies to their present state.

When tragic characters bring the past forward, they do so with an eye to the dramatic present, a subject discussed in Chapter 3. When Tecmessa appeals to Ajax, for example, she tells the story of her past (and her possible future) in order to influence her husband's behaviour *now*. Tecmessa is not exceptional in this regard; many tragic figures face the present and future by refusing to forget the past. Of course, characters can disagree violently about prior events and their relevance. Ajax doesn't listen to Tecmessa, for example – but we do. Hecuba and Helen, Medea and Jason, Agamemnon and Clytemnestra offer different views of the past, disclosing it as a site of conflict and contestation, as well as of causality and perceived order. But the past remains of crucial importance to what lies ahead, and those who don't know, ignore, or forget their past sooner or later run into it. We find a similarly agonistic, controverted sense of history in Herodotus and Thucydides, the 'inventors' of the genre. Over the course of the fifth century, Athenians became increasingly interested in the connections between past and present, and their impact on a volatile future.

Myth imbues the tragic world with the importance of priority, with what 'came before', and this deep valuation of the past (even when it provides a negative example) works as a brake on the race to tomorrow. Tragedy's caution towards the future admits a paradox that many of us prefer to forget: the future's dependency on – and frequent repetition of – the past, coupled with its vast uncertainty. As Theseus, the ruler of Athens, observes in *Oedipus at Colonus*, 'I know that I am human and that/ I have no greater share in tomorrow than you' (*OC* 567-8). Theseus understands his past as present ('I am human'), and this awareness allows him to see his uncertain place in all that lies ahead.

The priority of the past in Greek tragedy is not about nostalgia, or the desire to escape to an easier time, or a psychological fear of the unknown. On the contrary, as the plays demonstrate, tragic characters turn to the past in order to influence – 'flow into' – the future. At the same time, the tragedians placed their mythic heroes in a world that reflected fifth-century Athenian concerns, a temporal crossover discussed in Chapter 4. Political and cultural anachronisms brought the mythic world out of the past and into the present of those gathered in the theatre of Dionysus. The complex interplay between then and now vitalized the audience's sense of the choices that lay before them.[22] We find this dialectic between temporal rootedness and freedom in other innovations of the fifth century – architecture, sculpture, politics, philosophy, social thought – that continue to challenge us today.

In the modern world, we face a heavy (and heavily advertised)

138

onslaught of the 'now' and an incessant privileging of the immediate future. We are discouraged from studying history, especially that for which we bear any responsibility, and we are rewarded for finding old things 'dated', old-fashioned, boring, or irrelevant, unless they can be repackaged as nostalgia or recycled as novelties for a new run at the market. Otherwise, holding on to the old impedes our desire to purchase the new, unwelcome in a consumerist society like the United States. By its manifold untimeliness, therefore, Greek tragedy offers (minimally) some 'perspective by incongruity' (as Kenneth Burke puts it), its temporal 'otherness' refracting our parochial, market-driven sense of time.

To be sure, buying and selling do not adequately capture the complexities of modern temporality, but they explain a lot. The discussion by Marx (and other left-wing socialists) of alienated labour and commodity fetishism reveals much about capitalism and its cultural discontents. We sell our social and personal time to those who control the means of production, from fast-food chains like McDonald's to the coal fields, from IBM and Microsoft to the mass media, from drug companies to agricultural conglomerates. In exchange, we receive money (wages, salaries, tips) that allows us to live our 'real life', which usually amounts to consuming the very products, images, and ideas that we are paid to produce or service. The process has become so habitual that we cannot imagine a system different from 'wage slavery', as critics call it with only slight hyperbole. Greek tragedy says nothing about such economic processes, outside of general warnings against the corrupting influences of wealth, money, and power. But its focus on the relationship of past to future, and its portrayal of wider temporal contexts, suggests tragedy's radical distance from the 'time is money' mentality that defines our modern world and influences much of its art.

Epilogue

Progress and Survival

We can point to Greek plays that show advances over time – the *Oresteia*, for example – but tragedy generally does not subscribe to a 'progress model', as discussed in Chapter 3. The novelist and art critic John Berger distinguishes cultures of progress (which envisage ever-increasing future expansion) from peasant societies (which acknowledge scarcity as a basic fact of survival). Those who work the land take their ideals from the past and work to meet their obligations to the future (animals, crops, families, debt), part of the cyclical temporality that informs traditional societies until their members are uprooted, forced or seduced to join the sprawling shanty towns that ring the world's great cities. Removed from the land, cut off from the past, excluded from the benefits of progress, and abandoned by tradition, these transplanted peasants represent little more than labour fodder for those who have organized the world for their own benefit.

Berger links this attack on traditional societies to the temporal dominance of capitalist ideology:

> [T]he historic role of capitalism ... is to destroy history, to sever every link with the past and to orientate all effort and imagination to that which is about to occur. Capital can only exist as such if it continually reproduces itself; its present reality is dependent on its future fulfilment. This is the metaphysic of capital. The word *credit*, instead of referring to a past achievement, refers only in this metaphysic to a future expectation. How such a metaphysic eventually came to inform a world system, how it has been translated into the practice of consumerism, how it has lent its logic to the categorization of those, whom the system impoverishes, as backward (i.e., bearing the stigma and shame of the past) is beyond the scope of this essay.[1]

The answers to Berger's closing questions also lie beyond the scope of this book, but if the approach adopted here has merit, then Greek tragedy stands as a potential form of cultural resistance against the temporal compulsions of capitalism.

We should linger a moment on the simple fact of tragedy's survival. That any Greek plays have come down to us at all reflects the remarkable work of 'text-driven' grammarians, scribes, scholiasts, copyists, papyrologists, textual critics and editors. Without their efforts, the plays would have been lost long ago, and with them the many performances that have followed since the original productions of fifth-century Athens. Here we should keep in mind the observation of contemporary director Michael Blakemore, a man of the stage and not the library: 'What endures? The play on the page. The most perfect production, no less than the most flawed, is doomed to extinction.'[2]

The idea of survival, of course, requires that the past continues into the future. And it is surely worth noting what things have managed to survive, and what have not. In addition to a myriad of individual beings, entire languages, cultures, cities, peoples, forests, prairies, lakes, rivers, glaciers and biological species have disappeared since the time of the Greeks. As human invention advances, and our intervention in the processes of nature (including our own) accelerate, the moral compulsion to guarantee the survival of the past should grow accordingly. There are countless issues more important than the vitality of Greek tragedy. But by focussing on its radical potential, I have tried to show how tragedy's survival might help us with our own.

Notes

Introduction

1. From the *Preface to The Use and Abuse of History*, tr. A. Collins (New York 1949; orig. 1873-74) 12.

2. Diamond 1996, 2.

3. See, e.g., Diamond 1996, 4-5; Butler 1993, 95, 243; Helbo 1991, 12.

4. Derrida 1982 (esp. 'Signature Event Context'); Butler 1990, 1993; Parker and Sedgwick 1995, 2.

5. Carlson 1996 offers a magisterial survey and analysis, marred only by his deference to the field when he self-reflexively wonders 'what sort of performance was involved in this process of writing about performance' (187). This gesture has become *de rigueur*. Diamond 1996, 7-8, for example, proposes 'to stage a dialogue between performance and cultural studies ... [where] the critique of performance merges with the performance of critique'. In a shadow move, Goldhill (in Goldhill and Osborne 1999) entitles his introduction 'Programme Notes'.

6. Sokal and Bricmont 1998, esp. 124-35 and 261-3; P. Boghossian, 'What the Sokal hoax ought to teach us,' *TLS*, 13 December 1996, 14-15.

7. For a clear-headed account of deconstructionist misreadings of Saussure, see Tallis 1995, and J. Drake, 'The Naming Disease', *TLS*, 4 September 1998, 14-15. For analyses of the wider problem, see M.J. Devaney, *'Since at Least Plato' ... and Other Postmodernist Myths* (New York 1997), and C. Norris, *The Truth about Postmodernism* (Oxford 1993) and *What's Wrong With Postmodernism* (Baltimore 1990).

8. See J.R. Searle, 'Reiterating the Differences: A Reply to Derrida', *Glyph* 1 (1977) 198-208. For an overview of the influence of 'post-Saussurean' linguistics on performance theory, see Carlson 1996, 56-75. T. Gould, 'The Unhappy Performative' in Parker and Sedgwick 1995, 19-44, applies Austin's speech-act theory to Sophocles' *Antigone*.

9. In analysing his 'social dramas' (Turner 1969 and 1974) – which include any change of status, rank, stable position, place, occupation, normal behavior, state (even, it seems, of mind) – Turner expands van Gennep's triadic structure into a four-fold scheme: (1) a breach of normal social relations; (2) a subsequent crisis; (3) redressive action; (4) reintegration (1974, 38-41). What this scheme explains or elucidates is sometimes hard to tell. Schechner's 'restored behaviour' (Schechner 1985, 55) possesses a similar non-discriminating *largesse*: 'Performance behavior is known and/or practised behavior – or "twice-behaved behavior," "restored behavior" ....' By this definition, brushing one's teeth constitutes performance behaviour, as does

143

an actor playing King Lear, or a bombardier dropping napalm. For an excellent summation of Turner's and Schechner's theatre anthropology (and its limits), see Ley 1999, 141-210.

10. See, e.g., F. Jameson, *The Cultural Turn: Selected Writings on the Postmodern, 1983-1998* (London 1998). Blau 1992, 12 observes 'the apparent theatricalization of everything in sight: fashion, therapy, politics, lifestyle'. Never far behind, Madison Avenue offers a recent fashion advertisement (in the *New York Times*) featuring a sexy woman, dressed for today, and the text:

> Taking no stand,
> I let things stand for themselves
> Like water, I move along
> Like a mirror, I reflect
> Like an echo, I respond
> *ZOZA* Urban Performance Clothing

Performance clothing?

11. See L. Irigaray, *The Sex Which Is Not One*, tr. C. Porter (Ithaca 1985); S. Suleiman, ed. *The Female Body in Western Culture: Contemporary Perspectives* (Cambridge, Mass. 1986); S.-E. Case, ed. *Performing Feminisms: Feminist Critical Theory and Theatre* (Baltimore 1990); Butler, 1990 and 1993; S. Lurie, 'The "Woman" (in) Question: Feminist Theory and Cultural Studies', *Discourse* 14.3 (1992) 89-103; M. Garber, *Vested Interests: Cross Dressing and Cultural Anxiety* (New York 1992); J. Dolan, *Presence and Desire: Essays on Gender, Sexuality, Performance* (Ann Arbor 1993); L. Hart, *Acting Out: Feminist Performance* (Ann Arbor 1993); Elin Diamond, *Unmaking Mimesis: Essays on Feminism and Theater* (London 1997); L. Goodman, *Sexuality in Performance: Replaying Gender in Theatre and Culture* (London 1998). Even archaeology becomes a performance; see M. Shanks and M. Pearson, *Theatre/Archaeology* (London 2001).

12. Schechner quoted in Phelan and Lane 1998, 357-62. As Schechner put it a decade earlier (1988, 283), 'Performativity – or commonly "performance" – *is everywhere* [orig. emphasis] in life, from ordinary gestures to macro-dramas'.

13. '*Performance theory* is a social science, not a branch of aesthetics. I reject aesthetics' (Schechner 1973, vii). For those under the spell of the 'postmodern condition', as Blau (1992, 12) points out, 'the "superfetation of image" in the age of simulacra confirmed once more the mere redundancy of theater'.

14. We find a good example of this kind of theatrical theorizing in Barbara Freedman, *Staging the Gaze: Postmodernism, Psychoanalysis and Shakespearian Comedy* (Ithaca 1991) 66:

> On the side of neither presence nor absence, theater stages a continual posing and reposing of the interplay of regards .... This strategic decentering challenges the distinction between observer and observed, eye and gaze, and so suggests the power of theater as theory.

15. Theory as theatre effectively flips Diderot's *The Actor's Paradox* on its head. Diderot asks us to 'reflect for a moment on what one calls in the theatre *being true*. Is this to show things there as they are in nature? Not at all. Truth in this sense would be nothing more than commonplace' (Diderot 1957, 23; orig. *c.* 1784).

16. On the Renaissance 'memory theatres' of Giulio Camillo (1480-1544) and Robert Fludd (1574-1637), see Yates 1966, 129-59 and 320-41. In the theatre itself, Jacques in Shakespeare's *As You Like It* (2.7) asserts, 'All the world's a stage,/ And all the men and women merely players', and Macbeth concludes that 'Life's but a walking shadow, a poor player/ That struts and frets his hour upon the stage/ And then is heard no more' (*Macbeth* 5.5). Calderón de la Barca's *El Gran Teatro del Mundo* (*The Great Theatre of the World*) and *La Vida es Sueño* (*Life is a Dream*) also play on the illusory, theatrical nature of life, a popular theme in seventeenth-century Spanish drama.

17. S. Goldhill ('Programme Notes'), in Goldhill and Osborne 1999, esp. 1-10.

18. Ley 1999, 20-1 emphasizes the difference between the imitation and its model: '*mimêsis* is used of something that is known and/or acknowledged not to be what it shows itself to be, what it cannot possibly be.' This observation reflects what Samuel Johnson put succinctly, 'The delight of tragedy proceeds from our consciousness of fiction; if we thought murders and treasons real, they would please no more' (from 'Preface to Shakespeare', quoted in Nuttall 1996, 17). Nonetheless, the idea of similarity (between the fiction and the reality) *also* motivates the use of the term, as the *Heracles* examples indicate. This inherent tension empowers *mimêsis* to inspire, shock, predict, and explain.

19. See *Delian Hymn to Apollo* 163; Aeschylus *Cho.* 564, frs 57 (l. 9) and 364 (Nauck, 2nd edn), and fr. 276 (l. 7, in Smyth and Lloyd-Jones 1957; see also P. O'Sullivan, 'Satyr and Image in Aeschylus' *Theoroi*', *Classical Quarterly* 50 [2000], 353-66); Pindar *P.* 12.21 and fr. 94b; Democritus DK 68 B39; Herodotus 5.67; Euripides *Hipp.* 114, *Hel.* 74-5, *Rh.* 255 (on authenticity of *Rhesus* see p. 161 n.12); Aristophanes *Thesm.* 156 and 850, *Pl.* 291; Plato *Resp.* 3.392d, 393c-d (*mimêsis* as 'making oneself like another either in voice or bearing'), 394d (*mimêsis* linked directly to tragedy and comedy), 10.603c ('mimetic compositions imitate men carrying out actions'), 604e-605e. See also Nehamas 1999, 257-60; Nagy 1996 (4, 52-8, 80-6, 214) and 1989, 47-51; Kosman 1992; Ricoeur 1984, 32-8, 48 (*mimêsis* as 'mimetic' or 'representative *activity*'); and Else 1958, who gathers relevant passages (79-82). Cf. Ley 1999, 17-21, who tries to distinguish the pre-Platonic sense of the term from 'performance' understood in a theatrical context, claiming (wrongly I believe) that Plato made 'a radical linguistic decision' (21) in applying *mimêsis* to direct speech in epic and to performance in general. As for the ancient use of *mimêsis* for music, recall that *mousikê* usually meant the performance of poetry to musical accompaniment, and that certain melodies and modes (according to Aristotle, e.g. *Pol.* 8.5 [1339a-b] and 8.7 [1341b-42a]) could 'imitate' moral states such as courage or anger. See also Herington 1985, 3-40 ('Poetry as a Performing Art'), and Sifakis 2002, 158-60.

20. Nehamas 1999, 264, who debunks two common misreadings of Plato's view of *mimêsis* in *Republic*: (1) that Plato accuses art of being an imitation of an imitation, and (2) that Plato banishes the artists, or art in general, from his ideal state. Regarding the first, 'nothing in the text implies that the relationship between a work of art and its subject is the same as that between a physical object and its Form or Forms' (Nehamas 1999, 261-4). As for the second, Plato banishes only *dramatic poetry* from his republic. Painting definitely remains, and artists *per se* garner little attention (251, 264-9, 280-90).

21. Musical competitions were especially prominent at the Pythian games in Delphi. See West 1992, 19-20 and 336-8; Parke 1977, 34-5 (on the Panathenaia); and Kemp 1966 (professional musicians in ancient Greece). For the close link between Greek sport and music, see W. Decker, *Sport in der griechischen Antike* (Munich 1995) 61.

22. See Herington 1985, 10-15 and 51-4. On rhapsodes, see Plato's *Ion*, newly translated in *Classical Literary Criticism*, ed. P. Murray (London & New York 2001).

23. On the dithyramb, see Arist. *Po*. 1449a9-13; on the influence of epic, *Po*. 1448a1-30, 1448b28-1449a2, 1449b9-20, and 1460a5-26; also 1451a16-29, 1459a17-b32, and 1461b26-end.

24. See, e.g., Wiles 2000, 168-70, and Ford 1995, 127 ('The *Poetics* ... makes possible a new literary genre, the theory of literature').

25. Performance unnecessary – Arist. *Po*. 1450b19 (also 1450a15-b3); visual elements nonessential – 1450b20 (also 1462a11-17); importance of plot – 1450b3 (also 1450a15-b4, 1453b1-8); translations by Else 1970. Note, however, that Aristotle insists that a good tragic poet should visualize the scene when composing it (*Po*. 1455a21-29); see Ley 1999, 46-51 and Halliwell 1998, 337-43 (on Aristotle's equivocation regarding drama in the theatre), and Sifakis 2002 (on Aristotle and the actor).

26. See Arist. *Po*. 1456a26-32 and 1461b26-62a11; Page 1934, 15-105; Salkever 1986, 302-3; and Green 1994, 49-64. As Nehamas 1999, 279-99 ('Plato and the Mass Media') notes, when Plato wished his ideal city free from dramatic poetry, he was taking on the fourth-century BCE equivalent of commercial television. For a contrary view, see Csapo 2002, 129-31.

27. St John Wilson 1989, 67.

28. For further observations on this issue, see W.R. Johnson, *Lucretius and the Modern World* (London 1999).

29. Vernant 1972, 285. See Chapter 3.

30. On (1), see M. Fried, 'Art and Objecthood', in G. Battcock ed., *Minimal Art* (New York 1968) 116-47 (esp. 127-47, where Fried champions art that is *only* present, escaping both duration and context); on (2), P. Phelan, 'The Ontology of Performance: Representation without Reproduction', in *Unmarked: The Politics of Performance* (London 1993) 146-66 ('Performance's being ... becomes itself through disappearance'); J. Féral, 'Performance and Theatricality: The Subject Demystified', *Modern Drama* 25 (1982) 170-81 (unlike traditional theatre, 'performance' offers 'nothing to grasp, project, introject, except for flows, networks, and system. Everything appears and disappears like a galaxy of "transitional objects" representing only the failures of representation'). On (3), see Derrida 1982 and Butler 1993, 94, which she reiterates in J. Butler, E. Laclau, and R. Laddager, 'The Uses of Equality', *Diacritics* 27 (1997) 10:

The failure of any subject formation is an effect of its iterability, its having to be formed in time, again and again. One might say, via Althusser, that the ritual through which subjects are formed is always subject to a rerouting or a lapse by virtue of this necessity to repeat and reinstal itself.

31. Derrida 1982, 135; J. Erickson, 'The Spectacle of the Anti-Spectacle: Happenings and the Situationist International', *Discourse* 14 (1992) 36-58 (spectacle as the apotheosis of the commodity form, the 'vacuous incarnation of capitalism itself'); G.J. Lischka, 'Performance Art/Life Art/Mediafication', same vol. 124-41 (performance art escapes, performance never does); and generally Carlson 1996, 165-86 ('Resistant Performance').

32. Discussing 'Postmodernity and Contemporary Social Thought', in *Politics and Social Theory*, ed. P. Lassman (New York 1989) 158, Wayne Hudson draws the obvious conclusion:

Much of the current discussion is an in-house dialogue between Anglo-American and Franco-German philosophical and literary cultures, a dialogue in which having read Derrida or Heidegger or Wittgenstein or Adorno is much more important than understanding the world economy or having experience of famine in Africa.

1. Theatre, Artifice, Environment

1. As Artaud insists (1958, 37), 'the stage is a concrete physical place which asks to be filled, and to be given its own concrete language [i.e. gesture, not speech] to speak'. Grotowski (1968, 15) describes his 'poor theatre' as a *via negativa* that eliminates many elements we associate with modern theatre, but not the indoor theatrical spaces provided in Opole and Wroclaw, Poland. See also Schechner 1973, where the 'environmental' theatre of the Performance Group stays indoors.

2. Wycherley 1962, 161-2 and 171. For photographs and plans of the theatre of Dionysus showing its openness to the surrounding environment, see Rehm 2002, figs 1-6.

3. Barthes 1985, 79; see also Wiles' useful observations (2000, 113-14).

4. A. *Ag.* 1-24, *PV* 88-95; Eur. *El.* 54, 102, *Ion* 82-8, *Ph.* 1-6, *Alc.* 244-5 (Alcestis' first appearance), *Med.* 56-8 (the Nurse speaks of Medea's troubles 'to the earth and sky'), and 148 (the Chorus call on 'Zeus, and earth, and daylight'); S. *Tr.* 96-101, *Ant.* 100-9, *El.* 17-22 (Tutor) and 86-91, 103-9 (Electra's first appearance). Such invocations do not imply that the performances started at dawn, unlikely given the realities of ancient travel and the logistics of accommodating an audience of roughly 12,000-14,000 people.

5. The same applies to Oedipus in Sophocles' last play (*OC* 1549-52) and Iphigenia in Euripides' *Iphigenia in Aulis*, who speaks these lines as she leaves to die:

> Ah look! look! [*iô iô*]
> torch-bearing day and
> divine light! To a different
> life, a different fate [*moiran*] I go to dwell.
> Farewell, precious light. Ah look!
> Euripides *Iphigenia in Aulis* 1505-9

For Hades as unseen, see Pl. *Phd.* 81c and *Crat.* 404b.

6. Oaths and appeals to the sun occur at *Medea* 148, 746, 752, 1251-2, 1258, and 1326-8.

7. Thucydides 2.15.3.

8. Zeitlin 1990, 131, an argument adopted by many scholars. For a useful corrective, see Croally 1994, 38-42, 188-91, 205-7, and 213-14. Note, for example, that the Athenian leader Theseus in Sophocles' *Oedipus at Colonus* distinguishes the good city of Thebes from its evil ruler Creon (*OC* 919-23), expressing surprise that enmity could spread from there to Athens (*OC* 606).

9. Although the date of *Oedipus Tyrannus* remains uncertain, most scholars agree on 429-425 BCE, coinciding with the outbreak and recurrence of the epidemic in Athens. Of course, circularity here is unavoidable. See Knox 1979 (orig. 1956) 112-24. Cf. C.W. Müller, *Zur Datierung des sophokleischen Oedipus* (Wiesbaden 1984), who dates the play to 434, before the outbreak of the Peloponnesian War and the plague.

10. The quotations in order are Thuc. 1.23, 2.47-54, and 3.87; translations by Wick/Crawley, *The Peloponnesian War* (New York 1982).

11. Jebb 1888 on *OT* 20. 'Pallas' is another name for the goddess Athena, whose two most important shrines on the Athenian Acropolis were 'of the city' (*Polias*) and for 'the maiden' (*Parthenos*).

12. Knox 1957, 78-93; G. Greiffenhagen, 'Der Prozess des Oedipus: Strafrechtliche und strafprozessuale Bemerkungen zur Interpretation des *Oedipus Rex*', *Hermes* 94 (1966) 147-76; and R.G. Lewis, 'The Procedural Basis of Sophocles' *Oedipus Tyrannus*', *Greek, Roman, and Byzantine Studies* 30 (1989) 41-66.

13. Havelock 1982, 293-9 (quotation at 295), supported by Rosenbloom 1993, 188-90. Another Persian invasion remained a real possibility until Cimon's victory at Eurymedon, probably the year after *Seven* was first performed. See Meiggs 1972, 75-86. The historical Thebes actually 'medized' (supported Persia) during the Persian Wars, a source of later embarrassment for the city and a pretext for its destruction in 335 BCE by Alexander the Great.

14. Pickard-Cambridge 1968, 58.

15. Webster 1967, 205-11; fr. 182a (Nauck-Snell 1964); see also Nightingale 1995, 69-87 on the use of Euripides' *Antiope* in Plato's *Gorgias*.

16. Dillon 1997.

17. See A. Nightingale, *On Wondering and Wandering: Theôria in Greek Philosophy and Culture* (Cambridge, forthcoming).

18. See McAuley 1999, 262-3. Explaining why the Guthrie Theatre chose an open-stage configuration over a proscenium arch, Tyrone Guthrie (in 1963) noted the latter's resemblance to the flattened TV and film screen ('the rectangular postcard shape which has become the symbol of canned drama'), inadequate for staging the classics, which demand a more fully three-dimensional treatment (quoted in Izenour 1977, 603).

19. In absurdist plays like Ionesco's *The Bald Soprano*, the humour depends on realist conventions. The clock may strike 27, but it doesn't fly off, and the walls of the room stay vertical.

20. Aristotle *Poetics* 1450a38-9. See Hegel's invaluable analysis (1962, *passim*, but esp. 36-96); Bradley's 1901 lecture 'Hegel's Theory of Tragedy', in Bradley 1941, 69-95 (esp. 76-87); and Auerbach 1953, 318-25. As Tennessee Williams wrote in a 1939 letter, 'I have only one major theme for all my work which is the destructive impact of society on the sensitive, nonconformist individual'. Nothing could be further from the spirit of Greek tragedy.

21. See P.E. Easterling in Easterling, ed. 1997, 211-27; Csapo and Slater 1995, 14-17; O. Taplin, *Comic Angels and Other Approaches to Greek Drama through Vase-Painting* (Oxford 1993).

22. As Sir Frank Kermode puts it, 'a canonical [i.e. 'classical'] text does not want to clarify itself' ('Wholeness', lecture delivered at the Stanford Humanities Center, 14 November 2001).

23. For the 'found object' and 'sausage' metaphors, see R. Beacham, 'John Barton Directs the Greeks', *Theater* 11 (no. 3, 1979) 37. See also Hardwick 2000. This 'catch-all' attitude reflects postmodern lack of interest in plot and narrative form, epitomized by Brian Eno ('rock-musician-producer-philosopher', according to *NY Times*, 20 September 2001):

> An artist is now much more seen as a connector of things, a person who scans the enormous field of possible places for artistic attention, and says 'What I am going to do is draw your attention to this sequence of things.' .... Your story might involve foot-binding, Indonesian medicine rituals and late Haydn string quartets, something like that. You have made what seems to you a meaningful pattern in this field of possibilities .... To create meanings... *is* to create.
>
> Interview in *Wired*, May 1995, 207

24. Lévi-Strauss 1963, 206-31.

25. Black 1999, 308-13. Ranald 1984, 174 concludes that 'with this play, O'Neill establishes himself as a playwright of genius', disproving the claim 'that tragedy is impossible of achievement by modern playwrights'. We might contrast O'Neill's take on Greek tragedy with that of the recent musical comedy *Io! Princess of Argos!* (an adaptation based on Aeschylus' Io in *Prometheus Bound*). According to author-director Mark Jackson, 'Io's a person with a lot of questions about what life is supposed to mean .... She achieves a comfort level asking the question why and never getting an answer' (*San Francisco Arts Monthly*, April 2002, 2). Such banalities make O'Neill look positively Greek.

26. 'Dramatic text' has ramifying meanings, one of which involves what Adolphe Appia calls the 'theatrical form [of the text or score], i.e. its projection in space', a view shared by Gordon Craig (see Beacham 1987, 18 and 107-11). Tony Harrison, theatre poet and translator of the *Oresteia*, describes Aeschylus' language as 'fledged to fill the theatre', powerful 'like a strong current moving great boulders' (Symposium on the Contemporary Performance of Ancient Greek and Roman Drama, 20-23 June 2002, J. Paul Getty Museum, Los Angeles). Harrison emphasizes the link between Aeschylean language (in its operative sense) and the energies of nature, but we shouldn't forget the civic and public issues embedded there as well.

2. Tragedy and Fear

1. Rosenbloom 1993, 187. On the Spartans' cult of *Phobos*, see N. Richer in A. Powell and S. Hodkinson, eds, *Sparta: New Perspectives* (London 1999).

2. See Hutchinson 1985, xxxiii-xxxvii.

3. See Mastronarde 1994 on 361 for other examples of such fearful doubling.

4. See especially Lazenby 1991.

5. Thucydides 5.71.1; Lazenby 1991, 91; Rood 1998, 98; and generally V.D. Hanson, *The Western Way of War* (orig. New York 1989; augmented repr. Berkeley 2000). Close-proximity warfare also could extend to naval engagements, where each trireme carried a complement of hoplite marines.

6. See J. Keegan, *The Face of Battle* (New York 1976), on the differences between ancient and modern warfare. In this light we might consider the 'lessons' from the Vietnam War adopted by US policy makers: a preference for 'low-intensity' conflict carried out by proxies (US-trained and funded military and paramilitary troops, or disaffected nationals armed and en-camped outside the country, like the Contras based in Honduras and Costa Rica that killed some 10,000 Nicaraguan civilians between 1981 and 1989); increased domestic security and intelligence surveillance; severe limitations on press access to combat zones (the 'news blackout' during the 1990 Gulf War and the war in Afghanistan); the use of heavy air bombardment and reluctance to commit US land forces (the Gulf War, Kosovo, Afghanistan); the elimination of the military draft, replaced by a professional army staffed by poorer segments of the population (as the epigraph to Chapter 4 suggests, joining the military is the only way that many US students can afford to attend college). See Chomsky 1987, 218-19, and 1994, 94-9. This policy extends to international treaties – for example, the US remains one of few nations that refuses to sign the Ottawa Convention prohibiting the use, stockpiling, production, and transfer of antipersonnel landmines.

7. The control of individual fear and cowardice for the sake of civic safety features prominently in Pericles' funeral oration (Thuc. 2.42.4).

8. Arist. *Rh*. 1382a21-3; 1382b32-4; 1386a24-6; Nehamas 1992, 296-7 and 300-1; Halliwell 1998, 175-83; and Konstan 2001, 49-74 and 128-36.

9. Lessing 1962 (orig. 1769), 176. Nehamas 1992, 302-3 draws a similar conclusion: 'My fear "for" Oedipus is in fact fear for me, though in a highly indirect and mediated manner.'

10. See Nuttall 1996; J. Lear, 'Katharsis', in Rorty 1992, esp. 326-35; S. Halliwell, 'Pleasure, Understanding, and Emotion in Aristotle's *Poetics*', in Rorty 1992, 241-60; and Golden 1976.

11. Arist. *Rh*. 1378a.

12. We might compare this passage from Euripides' lost *Kresphontes* (fr. 449, Nauck-Snell 1964): 'It would be better for us to gather together and lament/ a newborn infant, given all the evils he is entering.'

13. Taylor 1999, 51 (D160 and D161 = DK 68 B295 and B296). On children, Democritus observes that 'bringing up children is risky; even with good luck it is full of strife and worry, and with bad luck it is not exceeded by any other woe' (Taylor 1999, 45 [D139 = DK 68 B275]). Democritus concludes:

'I do not think that one should have children; for in having children I see many great dangers and much distress, and few blessings and those meagre and weak' (Taylor D140 = DK 68 B276).

14. Taylor 1999, 27 (D63 = DK 68 B199).

15. Evadne commits suicide by leaping onto her husband's funeral pyre in an ecstatic union with death in Euripides' *Suppliant Women*, and Menoeceus kills himself to save Thebes, fulfilling Teiresias' prophecy in *Phoenician Women*. Although they celebrate their self-inflicted deaths, their survivors feel the effects as total devastation. Cf. E.P. Garrison, *Groaning Tears: Ethical and Dramatic Aspects of Suicide in Greek Tragedy, Mnemosyne* Supp. 145 (Leiden 1995), who offers a far more positive reading of suicide in tragedy.

16. Despairing of her fate, Io contemplates suicide, prompting Prometheus to confront her with his own suffering, apparently endless because he can *never* die (A. *PV* 747-56). Inspired by Prometheus, and the fact that the future has not yet been written, Io overcomes her despair and faces what lies ahead.

17. Regarding *Oedipus Tyrannus*, de Romilly 1958, 19 concludes 'la crainte règne d'un bout à l'autre'.

18. For example, Oedipus' scene with Jocasta and the Corinthian Messenger (S. *OT* 973-1014) is riddled with expressions of terror. *Phobos* and related words occur at 974, 977, 980, 988, 989, 1002, and 1013; *oknos* (from *okneô*, 'shrink back from') and related words at 976, 986, and 1000; *tarbôn* at 1011; and *tremôn* at 1014.

19. Ion expresses the same sentiment, wondering how a ruler could think himself lucky or blessed if he always feared that someone might use violence against him to seize power (Eur. *Ion* 621-32).

20. For a reconstruction of the Danaid trilogy, see A.F. Garvie, *Aeschylus' Supplices: Play and Trilogy* (Cambridge 1969) esp. 163-233; H. Friis Johansen and E.W. Whittle, eds, *Aeschylus: The Suppliants I* (Copenhagen 1980) 47-55; and the useful summary by M. Ewans, ed. and tr. *Suppliants and Other Dramas* (London 1996) xxxix-l.

21. Waring 1999 offers a compelling overview and trenchant analysis.

22. Chomsky 1993, 206; P. Farmer, *The Uses of Haiti* (Monroe, Maine 1994) 267.

23. These include the 1961 Bay of Pigs invasion, various FBI and CIA plots against Cuban leaders, the bombardment of Cuban airwaves with US propaganda, federal funding and logistical support for the Cuban-American National Foundation (which has launched terrorist attacks from Miami against civilian targets in Cuba), a forty-year embargo against Cuba (1961-present), and the use of Camp Delta in Guantanamo Bay (a remnant of US colonialism) to imprison ostensible 'Al-Qaeda' members of the Taliban captured in Afghanistan, in violation of international law. See Chomsky 1994, 21-3 and 67-8, 1993, 143-54, and 1987, 71-4; Blum 1995, 184-93. The US embargo, coupled with other federal legislation forbidding various third-country trading with Cuba, has been condemned each year for the last ten years by the United Nations General Assembly, most recently in November 2001 by a vote of 167-3 (the three 'nay' votes from the United States, Israel, and the Marshall Islands). As a permanent member of the UN Security

Council, the US can veto any General Assembly resolution, rendering UN condemnations of the US embargo (illegal under international law) ineffective.

24. Figures from the UNHCR Statistical Report, Refugees (Population Data Unit, Population and Geographic Data Section), http://www.unhcr.ch. See also 'Introduction', *Amnesty International Annual Report* (2002).

25. Masterfully charted by de Romilly 1958, esp. 11-53.

26. See, for example, the bestsellers by G. de Becker, *The Gift of Fear* (New York 1998), and *Fear Less: Real Truth about Risk, Safety, and Security in a Time of Terrorism* (New York 2002).

27. For Aeschylus' linking of fear and premonition, see Sansone 1975, 46-51; fear is a prophet at A. *Cho.* 32-7 and 929.

28. See Poole 1987, 37-8; Lebeck 1971, 157 and 166; and generally C. Meier, *The Greek Discovery of Politics*, tr. D. McLintock (Cambridge, Mass. 1990; orig. Frankfurt am Main 1980). Sophocles' Menelaus (*Ajax* 1073-6) and Creon (*Antigone* 663-76) also stress the role that fear plays in preserving civic order.

29. See N. Demand, *Birth, Death, and Motherhood in Classical Greece* (Baltimore 1994) 71-86, and R. Garland, *The Greek Way of Life, From Conception to Old Age* (London 1990) 65-6.

30. Figures from United Nations Population Fund, Maternal Mortality (based on 1995 estimates), http://www.unfpa.org.

31. See Poole 1987, 227-8 and 239. Iphis' reaction verifies Pericles' observation in the funeral oration: 'We feel pain, not when deprived of goods we have not experienced, but when something we are used to is taken away' (Thuc. 2.44.2-3). The funeral oration written by Lysias (2.73) expresses sympathy for the parents of those who died fighting for Athens: 'What hardship could be more incurable than to bring forth and raise and then bury one's own children, and then face old age infirm in body, bereft of all hope, without loved ones, and with no means of support?'

32. For plot summaries of lost plays, see Lloyd-Jones 1996 (Sophocles), Webster 1967 (Euripides), Smyth and Lloyd-Jones 1957 (Aeschylus), and March 1998 (mythic background). Recall that fewer than 3% of fifth-century tragedies and satyr-plays survive.

33. See, for example, Seaford 1994, 344-69; Rose 1992, 185-265; Jean-Pierre Vernant, 'The Historical Moment of Tragedy in Greece', and Pierre Vidal-Naquet, 'Oedipus in Athens', both in Vernant and Vidal-Naquet 1988, 23-8 and 301-27.

34. On Yucca mountain and nuclear waste, see US Department of Energy documents at http://www.rw.doe.gov/progdocs and http://www.ymp.gov. For a less sanguine analysis, consult Citizen Alert, at http://www.citizenalert. org/yucca/index.html. For similar problems regarding nuclear waste in the UK, see the Royal Society's response to the Department for Environment, Food and Rural Affairs (DEFRA) consultation document 'Managing Radioactive Waste Safely', debunked as a PR ploy at www.royalsoc.ac.uk, summarized in WISE (World Information Service on Energy) and NIRS (Nuclear Information and Resource Service) *Nuclear Monitor* 568 (17 May 2002) 6-7. For a dramatist's view of Mutually Assured Destruction (MAD), see A. Kopit, *End of the World* (New York 1984).

35. See S. Freud, 'Some Character-Types met with in Psycho-analytic Work' (1915), in *On Creativity and the Unconscious*, ed. B. Nelson (New York 1958) 94-110 (esp. 94-107).

36. Sam Shepard, *Curse of the Starving Class*, Act 1 (in Shepard 1981, 152).

37. In U. Halfmann, ed. and comm., *Eugene O'Neill: Comments on the Drama and the Theater* (Tübingen 1987), p. 86 (Spring 1926) and p. 87 (April 1929).

38. M. Carr, *By the Bog of Cats* (Oldcastle, Ireland 1998).

39. In some versions of the myth, Medea kills her young brother Apsyrtus and throws his dismembered body *in seriam* overboard to slow her father's pursuing ship, enabling her and Jason to escape. Euripides alludes to the incident at *Medea* 166-7 and 1334.

40. For the importance of this principle in Greek thought, see Blundell 1989, 26-31 and Rehm 1994, 214 nn.1-4; in *Medea* specifically, see Rehm 1994, 146-9 and 214-16. Plato provides a representative view (*Meno* 71e), when Meno defines male virtue directly as 'helping friends and harming enemies'. In his funeral oration, Pericles emphasizes the motivational importance of this idea: 'None of these men put off the day of reckoning ..., for they wanted more to punish their enemies than to secure any personal blessings' (Thuc. 2.42.4).

3. The Fate of Agency, the Agency of Fate

1. Vernant 1972, 285, who concludes that such a question can be raised only when a man discovers he is not a free agent and yet must confront his actions. Vernant finds the tragic aspect of the problem precisely in this lack of agency, coupled with the need to take responsibility for one's actions. However, with no awareness of agency, or of agency violated, would Oedipus – to take the obvious case – acknowledge *any* relationship to the incest and patricide he unwittingly perpetrated? Compare Frye 1957, 212, who observes that 'the discovery ... which comes at the end of the tragic plot is not simply the knowledge by the hero of what has happened to him ... but the recognition of the determined shape of the life he has created for himself ...'. As for Orestes, this chapter suggests that the ethical mix of fate and agency is precisely the issue.

2. Jones 1962, 96-111 emphasizes the social and political reasons for Orestes' revenge, an important corrective to the modern cathexis on the character's psychological motivation.

3. Interestingly, the sermon on hell in James Joyce's *A Portrait of the Artist as a Young Man* (ed. C.G. Anderson, New York 1968 [orig. 1916] 122) has strong affinities with the living torment facing Orestes:

Every sense of the flesh is tortured and every faculty of the soul therewith: the eyes with impenetrable utter darkness, the nose with noisome odours, the ears with yells and howls and execrations, the taste with foul matter, leprous corruption, nameless suffocating filth, the touch of redhot goads and spikes, the cruel tongues of flame.

Divine punishment for human error and disobedience takes similar forms, although Joyce's version of a Catholic 'living' hell has qualities that no ancient Greek would ascribe to the afterlife.

4. Dodds 1951, 7, 16, 30-1. See the discussion by Winnington-Ingram 1980, 150-78 ('Fate in Sophocles').

5. Pylades speaks 'as if the god [Apollo] had possessed the seeming-mute and spoken through him' (Jones 1962, 102). As Antigone says in *Oedipus at Colonus*, 'If a god leads,/ no mortal can escape' (S. *OC* 252-3).

6. Lesky 1966, 80. We find a similar play on this paradox in Thucydides, explaining why the Peloponnesian War broke out: 'this necessary result came about by chance' (Thuc. 1.49.7).

7. Jones 1962, 126 compares the *Oresteia* to 'the strands of the spider's web whose whole slender frame is set trembling by a touch'.

8. With respect to Orestes' verdict, for example, we note that the US Supreme Court recently (24 June 2002) struck down as unconstitutional death sentences determined in states where juries had *not* participated in the sentencing process and in deciding whether the death penalty was applicable. This decision could affect the sentences of 168 condemned convicts now on death row in Arizona, Colorado, Idaho, Montana and Nebraska.

9. See Gouldner 1965; Lesky 1966; McIntyre 1981, 123-36; Easterling 1973 and 1990; Pelling 1990; Gaskin 1990; Williams 1993 (an essential contribution); Cairns 1993 (esp. Introduction and 139-46); and Nussbaum 2001. The quotation is from Stephen Greenblatt, *Marvelous Possessions* (Oxford 1991) 127.

10. The first quotation is from Gaskin 1990, 8; the second from Gouldner 1965, 114.

11. Dodds 1966, 42.

12. Dodds 1951, 1-63 provides the classic treatment of shame vs. guilt cultures, an account that Williams 1993 challenges in important ways.

13. Applying this insight to the end of the trilogy, Jones 1962, 112-13 reminds us that the trial of Orestes '*decides* something certainly; a verdict is reached, the knot is cut. But it solves nothing. The image of deadlock recovers its massive simplicity when we cease to believe that it is transcended.' To understand the depiction of progress in tragedy, we must not simply extract speeches *about* human progress – A. *PV* 442-506, S. *Ant.* 332-83 (the ode to Man), Eur. *Su.* 195-218 – and ignore the contexts in which they occur. On ancient notions of progress, see important discussions by Havelock 1957, 52-86 ('History as Progress'), Dodds 1973, 1-25, and Rose 1992, 185-305.

14. For etymologies, see Greene 1944, 402-3 (*moira*) and *RE* sv. 'Tyche' (G. Herzog-Hauser, vol. 7 [2] 1643-46). The concepts come together nicely in Euripides' *Iphigenia in Aulis* when Agamemnon cries out against 'powerful doom [*moira*] and fate [*tuchê*] and divine fortune [*daimôn*]', which compel him to sacrifice his daughter Iphigenia (Eur. *IA* 1136).

15. Greene 1944, 14; Dodds 1951, 6.

16. Redfield 1994, 131-2.

17. Quotation by Greene 1944, 90. The exchange between mother and son prior to the matricide epitomizes the revelatory nature of *moira* in tragedy. Accused of killing Agamemnon, Clytemnestra argues that 'Fate [*Moira*], my

son, shares the blame for that', to which Orestes responds, 'Then it is Fate [*Moira*] that works its doom against you' (A. *Cho.* 910-11).

18. Lebeck 1971, 49-50.

19. See E.J. Blakely and M.G. Snyder, *Fortress America: Gated Communities in the United States* (Brookings Institution, Washington, DC, 1997). On the explosion of prison construction and incarceration in the US (whose prison population rate – over 700 per 100,000 – is 5 times that of the UK, 20 times that of Japan), see C. Parenti, *Lockdown America: Police and Prisons in the Age of Crisis* (New York 1999); more generally, D. Garland, *The Culture of Control: Crime and Social Order in Contemporary Society* (Chicago 2001). Regarding Star Wars, the additional fact that its development and deployment sabotage hard-fought bilateral arms-control agreements proves that the 'national security' argument is a smokescreen. The Star Wars project stokes public faith in military technology, creating the illusion that it solves political and social problems. In the process, research, development and deployment help maintain the Pentagon system, which funnels public money into private corporations linked to the 'defence' business. The demonstrably false claims regarding the missile defence shield bear witness to the power of ideology, as the propaganda system repackages military and political dominance as 'minimal security needs'. See Greider 1999; Silverstein 1998, 187-220; Chomsky 1994, 100-13, 1992, 81-121, and 1987, 105-10; and Chapter 4, 'Tragedy and Ideology'.

20. See Lappé and Bailey 1998, 4-9, 33-72, 75-90, and 102-6; Magdoff et al. 2000, 107-23; Bello 2001, 18-32; Wilson 2002, 114-18. Under a form of corporate welfare, the US government subsidizes the export of genetically-modified corn and soybeans by offering it as 'food aid' to third world countries, not all of whom accept it. See Magdoff, etc. 2000, 125-43; N. Klein, 'Genetic Tampering', ZNET Commentaries, 25 June 2001, and V. Shiva, 'Biotech Companies as Bioterrorists', ZNET Commentaries, 6 November 2001 (on GM corn and cotton introduced by Monsanto in Gujarat in violation of Indian regulatory procedures), both available at http://www.zmag.org; and the recent rejection by Zambia of GM food 'donated' by the US to the World Food Program, whose food holdings are predominantly GMO (AP story by M. Mulenga, Friday 31 May 2002, *SF Chronicle* A15). We should also note the massive (and so far successful) lobbying effort by US agribusiness to stop federal legislation from requiring genetically-modified food to be labelled as such.

21. On designer babies, see 'Perfect? The ethics and politics of human cloning', *Economist*, 14-20 April 2001; 'Life Story, the Human Genome', Survey Supplement in the *Economist* by G. Carr, 1 July 2000, 1-16 (particularly 16); and Waring 1999, 179-80. For an invaluable response to the ethical challenges presented by these and other scientific advances, see P. Kitcher, *Science, Truth, and Democracy* (New York 2001). Artists have moved garishly into this brave new world. Consider Eduardo Kac's 'GFP Bunny' (1999), a live albino bunny designed for museum exhibition that glows bright green-yellow, an effect achieved by splicing the rabbit's DNA with that of a Pacific Northwest jellyfish. See 'Gene(sis): Contemporary Art Explores Human Genomics', Henry Art Gallery, University of Washington, Seattle (April-August 2002). Photo and story in *NY Times*, 26 May 2002 (Section 2, 1 and 30).

22. See Rood 1998, 78-82, 97-8, 224, 292-3 ('Thucydides suggests that ... our desire for safety deprives us of [moral and material] safety').

23. For an analysis of the commercialized aesthetic that results from the corporate takeover of art, see C. Wu, *Privatising Culture: Corporate Art Intervention Since the 1980s* (New York 2001).

24. Oedipus' death in Sophocles' *Oedipus at Colonus* provides the exception, although neither of his daughters is ready for the event.

25. On the Persian invasion, the evacuation of Athens, the sack of the city, and the eventual expulsion of the Persians from Greece, see Lazenby 1993.

26. The phrase is Kenneth Burke's, from *Language as Symbolic Action* (Berkeley 1966) viii.

27. See J. Chadwick, *Lexicographica Graeca* (Oxford 1998) 292-7; Cairns 1996; Fisher 1992, 1-6, 247-342, and 412-53 (who overemphasizes the role of the victim's dishonour and undervalues the outrage attached to the *perpetrator*).

28. See *LIMC* V.(1) 'Kapaneus', 952-63 and V.(2) figs 12-51. The image of a mortal struck down by the gods after rising too high recurs throughout Greek literature, from the *hubris* of Patroclus' assault on the walls of Troy that is stopped by Apollo (H. *Il.* 16.698-711, 786-805) to Pentheus' temporary erection in the tree above the Maenads, arranged by Dionysus with fatal consequences (Eur. *Ba.* 1064-75).

29. Winnington-Ingram 1983, 3. As Podlecki (1966, 8-26 and 125-9) and others point out, Aeschylus' emphasis on Athenian strategy and deception suggests tacit support for Themistocles, the mastermind of the victory at Salamis, who was ostracized for political reasons shortly after *Persians* was first performed.

30. C.J. Chivers, 'Two Worlds Paired by War', *NY Times*, 31 December 2001, B1 and B3 (quotation at B3).

31. In Aristotle's analysis, 'complex' tragic plots involve a reversal of fortune *either* from good to bad *or* from bad to good. See Arist. *Po.* 1453a (Else 1970, 35-9).

32. Examples are legion, perhaps none so dramatic as the largest industrial accident ever and the efforts by Union Carbide and Dow Chemical (which acquired UC in 2001) to deny liability. In 1984, a Union Carbide chemical plant in Bhopal, India released a cloud of methyl isocyanate, hydrogen cyanide, and other toxins, killing 4,000 to 8,000 people at the time, 16,000 in total, with 100,000 others suffering after-effects that continue to the present. An equally scandalous, though far less fatal, failure to accept executive responsibility involves the collapse of Enron, WorldCom, and other giant US-based multinationals, following news of falsified profit statements, questionable stock-option and market manipulation, CEO sweetheart packages, insider trading, and their role in human rights abuses. See Ritz ed. 2001, Frank 2000, Mokhiber and Weissman 1999, and Human Rights Watch 1999. We also should note the flight from principled action of government officials during the US Iran-Contra affair of the 1980s, and the BSE outbreak in the UK in the 1990s (particularly the Ministry of Agriculture, Fisheries and Food, who supported various agribusiness and animal feed companies at the expense of public safety).

33. It is for his actions (publicly there for others to see) rather than for his conduct (implying an interiority to which only he has access) that Oedipus deserves – and feels he deserves – to be punished. As Jones 1962, 37 points out, 'Aristotelian man cannot make a portentous gesture of "I have that within which passes show", because he is significantly himself only in what he says and does'. Dover 1974, 150-60 observes that, for the Greeks, divine reproach or punishment already signalled an agent's potential harm to the community, whatever the individual's motivations had been. Greek gods were not 'merciful', and the crime being punished – as our discussion of the *Oresteia* suggests – could well have a past that escapes immediate notice.

34. See E. Herman and F. Brodhead, *Demonstration Elections* (Boston 1984); Chomsky 1994, 49-67.

35. See Chomsky and Herman 2002; Chomsky 1987, 121-36, and 1992, 107-37 and 351-405.

36. Chomsky 1992, 64; see also his discussion of human freedom 1992, 397-401; 1987, 139-55 ('Language and Freedom', orig. 1970) and 183-202 ('Equality', orig. 1976); 1980, 3-46 ('Mind and Body').

4. Tragedy and Ideology

1. See Ober 1989, 38-52, and Kavanagh 1995. See also Féredi 1994; Chomsky 1994 (ideology as 'population control'); 1993 (on the 'ideological system'); 1987 (on power and ideology); Chomsky and Herman 1979 (on US imperial ideology); Lemisch 1975 (ideology and the writing of history).

2. The frequent comparisons to Pearl Harbor obscure crucial differences; see Mahajan 2002, 11-12. In 1941, the Japanese Air Force attacked a military base on an offshore colonial holding of the US empire, acquired by force in 1898.

3. Although statistics tell little of the story, it is worth noting that the 9/11 attacks killed just over 3,000 people. In the first nine weeks of the U.S. bombing of Afghanistan, M. Herold, economics professor at University of New Hampshire (in 'A Dossier on Civilian Victims of United States' Aerial Bombing of Afghanistan: A Comprehensive Accounting'), estimated the number of direct civilian casualties at 3,767, rising to 4,050 by January 2002 (*The Progressive*, February 2002, p. 9; Mahajan 2002, 47-51 and 83-6). This figure does not include thousands of deaths due to the massive increase in Afghan refugees (1.5 million, who fled to Pakistan and Iran) immediately preceding the US bombing campaign. Many of these succumbed to starvation or the elements. After the bombing began, the UN estimated that 7.5 million Afghans were at risk, because food shipments were stopped for several weeks. At that time, 6 million Afghans depended on UN food aid within Afghanistan, as well as 3.5 million living in refugee camps outside the country (*New York Times*, 25 September 2001). See also S. Ackerman, 'Afghan Famine On and Off the Screen', *Extra!*, May-June 2002, 7-8.

4. With almost an hour's warning the Pentagon failed to defend itself against a low-tech assault by a third domestic airliner. Contrast the effective action of citizens working in concert, who downed the fourth plane in Pennsylvania. See the analysis by Elaine Scarry, 'Nine, One, One: Citizenship in Emergency', Presidential Lecture in the Humanities, Stanford University, 25 February 2002.

5. Among many examples, we might consider the US-backed sanctions against Iraq, that have led to the deaths of over 1,000,000 civilians, more than half under the age of five (UN Food and Agriculture Organization [FAO] estimate in 1995, followed by UNICEF report 8/99); unconditional US support for Israel, in spite of its flouting UN resolutions, possession of weapons of mass destruction, flagrant violations of the Oslo accords, and brutal suppression of Palestinian rights; and US support for military-dominated governments that protect American investments (Guatemala, Indonesia, Colombia, and others).

6. It has become official doctrine that 9/11 represented an assault on America's 'democratic way of life'. Only the ideologically indoctrinated could swallow the claim that the businesses operating out of the WTC (including many major international investment and development firms) represented democratic institutions. See Mahajan 2002, 12-15.

7. On the US defence budget – at $434 billion for 2003, more than the combined total of *the next 25 nations* – see J.M. Cypher, 'Return of the Iron Triangle: The New Military Buildup', *Dollars and Sense* (January-February 2002), and 'Friends Committee on National Legislation Newsletter' 665 (April 2002) 2-3. The USA PATRIOT Act (the dismal acronym for 'Uniting and Strengthening America by Providing Appropriate Tools Required to Intercept and Obstruct Terrorism') threatens constitutional protections of free speech and free association (under its provisions, 'domestic terrorism' includes acts that 'appear to be intended to influence the policy of a government by intimidation or coercion'), and sanctions Justice Department 'roving surveillance'. See 'Justice Dept. Balks at Effort to Study Antiterror Powers', *New York Times*, 15 August 2002, A14. In addition, some 1,200 US immigrants have been held for months in 'preventative detention' with no charges brought against them and no legal redress available, violating constitutional guarantees of *habeas corpus*. See the American Civil Liberties Union website, www.aclu.org, and Mahajan 2002, 65-71.

8. On the Northern Alliance, see Rashid 2000, 21-40, and Cooley 1999, 80-125. As Amnesty International warned, 'By failing to appreciate the gravity of the human rights concerns in relation to Northern Alliance leaders, UK ministers at best perpetuate a culture of impunity for past crimes; at worst they risk being complicit in human rights abuse.' Quoted by J. Pilger, *Daily Mirror*, 16 November 2001.

9. In effect, 'terrorism' constitutes a useful excuse for the US to shore up its power at home and across the globe. 'Terrorists' serve the function once filled by 'communists', 'fellow-travellers', 'ultra-nationalists', 'rogue states', 'narco-traffickers', etc. See Mahajan 2002; Chomsky 1994 (54-61), 1988, and 1986; Herman and O'Sullivan 1989; Herman 1982; Chomsky and Herman 1979, 85-355.

10. In spite of state financial support – primarily through liturgies, a one-off tax on the rich (who paid for tragic, comic, and dithyrambic choruses) – we know of only two retroactive examples of theatrical censorship in fifth-century Athens. The tragedian Phrynichus was fined 1,000 drachmas for his play *Capture of Miletus*, based on the Persian sack of the Ionian city in 494 BCE, which Athens had done little to stop (see Rosenbloom 1993); in 426, the political demagogue Cleon charged that Aristophanes' comedy *Baby-*

Ionians (lost) had harmed the city. See S. Halliwell, 'Comic Satire and Freedom of Speech in Classical Athens', *Journal of Hellenic Studies* 111 (1991) 48-70.

11. Steiner 1984, 237.

12. Zeitlin 1996 and Foley 2001.

13. Quoted by Ian Watt in 'The Humanities on the River Kwai', 17, in *Critical History: The Career of Ian Watt*, ed. B. Thompson et al. *Stanford Humanities Review* 8 (2000).

14. Euripides is no sentimentalist, for when the old (male) slave learns of Xuthus' plan, he cannot bear the fact that Creusa will have to accept as her future master 'a motherless no-account sired off some slave girl' (838). The Tutor equates slave with free only as regards himself, not some *other* slave. The play exposes many such inconsistencies that challenge the social and cultural self-image of Athens. On the 'free vs. slave' issue, see P. Cartledge, *The Greeks* 2nd edn (Oxford 2002).

15. Thucydides 5.84-116.

16. NATO bombing of Kosovo and Serbia in 1999 increased ethnic tensions in the region and led to a vast increase in the number of Albanian refugees. President Clinton, Prime Minister Blair, and a parade of NATO spokesmen emphasized that the Kosovo campaign was necessary to establish the 'credibility of NATO', mouthing platitudes about NATO's responsibility to stop ethnic cleansing. However, neither Blair, Clinton, their predecessors, nor NATO took any significant action against the decades-long 'ethnic cleansing' that Turkey (a NATO member) has carried out against its own indigenous Kurdish population. See Chomsky 1999. Nor did concern for international human rights impede Britain and the United States in their ongoing diplomatic, military and economic support for the Suharto regime in Indonesia, which committed genocidal 'ethnic cleansing' in East Timor from 1975 to 1999, killing some 200,000 people, roughly one-third of the East Timorese population. Sadly, one can find other examples where NATO and its two most hawkish members have established 'credibility' in a similar fashion.

17. On US imperial interventions, see Blum 1995, Chomsky 1993 and 1988. The 'No War for Oil' slogan remains applicable today, vis-à-vis Iraq, and regarding US corporate plans for an oil pipeline through Afghanistan. See Rashid 2000, 143-82, and his interview in *Multinational Monitor*, November 2001, 20-1; also Klare 2001, 81-108, and his 'Oil Moves the War Machine', *Progressive*, June 2002, 18-19; and J-C. Brisard and G. Dasquié, *Forbidden Truth: US Secret Oil Diplomacy and the Hunt for Bin Laden* (New York 2002). The pipeline project helps explain the massive military effort to overthrow the Taliban government rather than to apprehend those responsible for the plane hijackings of 9/11. With a friendly government in Kabul, and military bases there and in Turkmenistan, Uzbekistan and Tajikistan, the US is poised to control the extensive oil production from the Caspian Sea, of long-term interest to the American oil company UNOCAL, which formerly employed the new president of Afghanistan, Hamid Karzai, as well as Zalmay Khalilzad, Washington's emissary to the new Afghani government. On 6 July 1997, the *Washington Post* reported that former US cabinet members and/or presidential advisers Gen. Brent Scowcroft, Zbigniew

Brzezinksi, John Sununu, James Baker and Richard Cheney [current Vice President] all had become oil and gas company executives involved in the Caspian region. Far from a conspiracy theory, these facts help to explain how ideology is useful in deflecting a meaningful analysis of the institutional forces that shape public policy.

18. See Rose 1992, Winkler and Zeitlin 1990, Podlecki 1966, among many others.

19. The translation is not excessive, as the 1912 rendition by A.S. Way indicates: 'the prater subtle-souled,/ the man of honied tongue, the truckler to the throng ....'

20. We should note that Athens plays an insignificant role in the Homeric stories of Troy. The sons of Theseus are Euripidean 'intrusions' on the myth.

21. See Rose 1992, 266-330.

22. See Rehm 2002, 310 n.144.

23. Pl. *Prt.* 326d; contrast Thucydides' Pericles (Thuc. 2.39).

24. Ion refers to the Athenian myth of autochthony, a relative latecomer in local legends, which claimed that the first Athenians sprang directly from the earth. Although scholars offer various interpretations of Athenian autochthony (from anti-maternal misogyny to racist fear of foreigners), the myth promoted democratic egalitarianism by 'levelling' citizens, since autochthonous Athenians could not owe their status to wealth or family. See Rehm 2002, 58-61 and bibliography at 327 (nn. 145 and 146).

25. Brecht 1974, 87 (orig. 1935). In a less lively vein, Augosto Boal (1985, 25) views the plot conventions of Greek tragedy as 'a form of oppression'. Although Boal's practical work on popular theatre remains inspiring and laudable, his reading of Greek tragedy and Aristotle's *Poetics* suggests he has not looked at either very closely. See Boal 1985, xi-xiv and 1-50 ('Aristotle's Coercive System of Tragedy').

26. Halliburton 1988, 265.

27. McChesney 2000; Bagdikian 2000; McChesney, Wood and Foster, eds 1998 (esp. 1-26 and 191-205); and Herman and McChesney 1997.

5. Tragedy and Time

1. A. Vitez, 'Témoignages', *Théâtres-Théâtre* 13 (May 1990) 5 (my translation).

2. Brook 1968, 138.

3. Dewey 1934, 214. His emphasis on the *work* that art does (and demands from us) suggests the loss that has resulted when literary theorists replaced the term 'work' with 'text'. See Rehm 2002, 8-12.

4. Time has meaning only *as* an event, although we tend to lose sight of this when we talk about time in the abstract. For Greek thinking about time as a non-abstract and affectively-charged phenomenon, see Lloyd 1976. On Greek measurement of time, see Rehm 2002, 276-7 with notes.

5. Pl. *Tim.* 37a; Arist. *Cael.* 1.9, 279a.

6. Kant 1998, 163: 'Time is nothing other than the form of inner sense, i.e., of the intuition of our self and our inner state.' The idea that 'time is logically prior to space' (H. Reichenbach, *The Philosophy of Space and Time* [New York 1958] 169) suggests that time is a mode of 'thinking' (being conscious of) duration, before it becomes a measure of different durations (days, hours, minutes, etc.).

7. Teiresias has already told Oedipus who he is, but the prophet does so in such a way that no one at the time – Oedipus, the Chorus, Creon, Jocasta – believes him.

8. Dewey 1934, 23-4.

9. In a fascinating exposition, Onians 1951, 343-8 defines *kairos* in terms of an 'opening'. Our word 'opportunity' shares a similar derivation from Latin: *ob* + *portunus*, 'toward a port or harbour'. This etymology points obliquely to the link between *tempestas* ('storm' or 'weather') and *tempus* ('time'), a subject explored in Shakespeare's *Tempest*.

10. Dewey 1934, 23.

11. See S.L. Higdon, *Time and English Fiction* (London 1977) 9-11.

12. Although we do not know how long the performance of an individual Greek tragedy took, scholars tend to overestimate it. The plays had no intermission; the ongoing presence of the Chorus provided continuity (only rarely did they leave the orchestra after their initial entrance and before their final exit); the longest Greek tragedy, *Oedipus at Colonus* (1779 lines) is less than half the length of *Richard III*, *Hamlet*, *Troilus and Cressida* or *Antony and Cleopatra*. *Eumenides* (at 1044 lines) is shorter than some Shakespearean 'acts'. Although attributed to Euripides, *Rhesus* at just under 1,000 lines may be a fourth-century tragedy.

13. A *'proemion'* (rhetorical introduction) also can occur in set speeches. Electra begins her tirade over the corpse of Aegisthus, 'How shall I start my speech of insult,/ and how end it? What key point should I put in the middle?' (Eur. *El.* 907-8).

14. A similar effect of leaving the temporal constraints of the plot occurs in the 'escape wish' of characters or Chorus who want to fly away from the impending crisis. See W.S. Barrett, ed. and comm., *Euripides, Hippolytus* (Oxford 1964) 297-9 (on *Hipp.* 732-52); also A. *Supp.* 792-9, and Eur. *Hel.* 1478-87.

15. On the high hopes the Athenians had for the Sicilian expedition, see Thuc. 6.8-26.

16. Their children included Erigone and Aletes; see March 1998 s.v.

17. At one point, Castor speaks as if the past working through Orestes and Electra has driven them from their homeland: 'Common actions, common fates./ The same curse from your ancestors/ has destroyed you both' (*El.* 1305-7). Outside of that moment, however, the family curse is ignored in the play.

18. Arrowsmith 1974, 3-21 calls this archetypal conflict 'modal' drama, a confusing name that does not weaken his insight into its operations.

19. The factors leading to these developments are many, including the impact of cinematic 'cutting' (intensified in MTV, rock videos, TV commercials, and feature films); the speed of personal computers and other technologies; the popularity of competitive sports with decisive outcomes; the avalanche of interest in gambling and gaming (lotteries, casinos, horse racing, team-sport betting, office pools, the stock market); a keen eye for the (quarterly) bottom line; and other modern provocations to immediate response and satisfaction.

20. For excellent discussions of anachronism in Greek tragedy, see Croally 1994, 207-48, and Easterling 1985.

21. See, e.g., L.E. Doherty, *Gender and the Intepretation of Classical Myth* (London 2001), and March 1998.

Epilogue

1. John Berger, *Pig Earth* (London 1992; orig. 1979) 195-213 ('Historical Afterword', quotation at 211).

2. *New Yorker*, 3 June 1996, p. 60.

Bibliography

Archer, L.J., ed. 1988. *Slavery and Other Forms of Unfree Labour* (London).

Arrowsmith, W., tr. and intro. 1974. *Euripides, Alcestis* (New York).

Artaud, A. 1958. *The Theater and its Double*, tr. M.C. Richards (New York).

Auerbach, E. 1953. *Mimesis: The Representation of Reality in Western Literature*, tr. W.R. Trask (Princeton; orig. 1942-45).

Bagdikian, B.H. 2000. *The Media Monopoly*, 6th edn (Boston).

Barthes, R. 1985. 'The Greek Theater': 63-88 in *The Responsibility of Forms*, tr. R. Howard (New York; orig. 1965).

Beacham, R.C. 1987. *Adolphe Appia, Theatre Artist* (Cambridge).

Bello, W. 2001. *The Future in the Balance: Essays on Globalization and Resistance*, ed. A. Mittal (Oakland).

Black, S.A. 1999. *Eugene O'Neill: Beyond Mourning and Tragedy* (New Haven).

Blau, H. 1992. 'The Prospect Before Us', *Discourse* 14:1-25.

Blum, W. 1995. *Killing Hope: US Military and CIA Interventions Since World War II* (Monroe, Maine).

Blundell, M.W. 1989. *Helping Friends and Harming Enemies: A Study in Sophocles and Greek Ethics* (Cambridge).

Boal, A. 1985. *Theatre of the Oppressed*, tr. C.A. and M.L. McBride (New York; orig. 1974).

Bradley, A.C. 1941. *Oxford Lectures on Poetry* (London; orig. 1909).

Brecht, B. 1974. *Brecht on Theatre: The Development of an Aesthetic*, ed. and tr. J. Willett, 2nd edn (New York; orig. 1918-56).

Brook, P. 1968. *The Empty Space* (New York).

Butler, J. 1990. *Gender Troubles* (New York).

———. 1993. *Bodies That Matter* (New York).

Cairns, D.L. 1993. *Aidôs: The Psychology and Ethics of Honour and Shame in Ancient Greek Literature* (Oxford).

———. 1996. 'Hybris, Dishonour, and Thinking Big', *Journal of Hellenic Studies* 116:1-32.

Carlson, M. 1996. *Performance: A Critical Introduction* (London).

Chomsky, N. 1980. *Rules and Representations* (New York).

———. 1986. *Pirates and Emperors* (Montreal).

———. 1987. *The Chomsky Reader*, ed. J. Peck (New York).

———. 1988. *The Culture of Terrorism* (Boston).

———. 1992. *Deterring Democracy* (New York).

———. 1993. *Year 501: The Conquest Continues* (Boston).

———. 1994. *World Orders, Old and New* (New York).

Bibliography

————. 1999. *The New Military Humanism: Lessons from Kosovo* (Monroe, Maine).

Chomsky, N. and Herman, E.S. 1979. *After the Cataclysm: Postwar Indochina and the Reconstruction of Imperial Ideology* (Boston).

————. 2002. *Manufacturing Consent: The Political Economy of the Mass Media*, 2nd edn (New York).

Cooley, J. 1999. *Unholy Wars: Afghanistan, America, and International Terrorism* (London).

Croally, N.T. 1994. *Euripidean Polemic: The 'Trojan Women' and the function of tragedy* (Cambridge).

Csapo, E. 2002. 'Kallippides on the Floor-sweepings: The Limits of Realism in Classical Acting and Performance Styles': 227-47 in Easterling and Hall.

Csapo, E. and Slater, W.J. 1995. *The Context of Ancient Drama* (Ann Arbor).

de Romilly, J. 1958. *Le crainte et l'angoisse dans le théâtre d'Eschyle* (Paris).

————. 1971. *Le temps dans la tragédie grecque* (Paris).

Derrida, J. 1982. *The Margins of Philosophy*, tr. A. Bass (Chicago).

Dewey, J. 1934. *Art as Experience* (New York; repr. 1980).

Diamond, E., ed. 1996. *Performance and Cultural Politics* (London).

Diderot, D. 1957. *The Paradox of Acting*, ed. L. Strasberg, tr. W.H. Pollock (New York; orig. *c*. 1784, first published 1830).

Dillon, M. 1997. *Pilgrims and Pilgrimages in Ancient Greece* (London).

Dodds, E.R. 1951. *The Greeks and the Irrational*, Sather Lectures vol. 25 (Berkeley; pbk 1971)

————. 1966. 'On Misunderstanding the *Oedipus Rex*', *Greece & Rome* 13:37-49 (= 1973, 64-77).

————. 1973. *The Ancient Concept of Progress* (Oxford).

Dover, K.J. 1974. *Greek Popular Morality in the Time of Plato and Aristotle* (Oxford & Berkeley).

Easterling, P.E. 1973. 'Presentation of Character in Aeschylus', *Greece & Rome* 20:3-19.

————. 1985. 'Anachronism in Greek Tragedy', *Journal of Hellenic Studies* 105:1-10.

————. 1990. 'Constructing Character in Greek Tragedy': 83-99 in Pelling.

————, ed. 1997. *Cambridge Companion to Greek Tragedy* (Cambridge).

Easterling, P. and Hall, E., ed. 2002. *Greek and Roman Actors: Aspects of an Ancient Profession* (Cambridge).

Else, G.F. 1958. 'Imitation in the Fifth Century', *Classical Philology* 53:73-90.

————, tr. 1970. *Aristotle, Poetics* (Ann Arbor).

Fisher, N.R.E. 1992. *Hubris: A Study in the Values of Honour and Shame in Ancient Greece* (Warminster).

Foley, H.P. 2001. *Female Acts in Greek Tragedy* (Princeton).

Ford, A. 'Katharsis: The Ancient Problem': 109-32 in Parker and Sedgwick 1995.

Frank, T. 2000. *One Market Under God: Extreme Capitalism, Market Populism, and the End of Economic Democracy* (New York).

Frye, N. 1957. *Anatomy of Criticism: Four Essays* (Princeton; repr. 1973).

Féredi, F. 1994. *The New Ideology of Imperialism* (London).

Bibliography

Gaskin, R. 1990. 'Do Homeric Heroes Make Real Decisions?', *Classical Quarterly* 40:1-15.

Golden, L. 1976. 'The Clarification Theory of Katharsis', *Hermes* 104:437-52.

Goldhill, S. and Osborne, R. ed. 1999. *Performance Culture and Athenian Democracy* (Cambridge).

Gouldner, A.W. 1965. *Enter Plato: Classical Greece and the Origin of Social Theory* (New York).

Green, J.R. 1994. *Theatre in Ancient Greek Society* (London).

Greene, W.C. 1944. *Moira: Fate, Good, and Evil in Greek Thought* (Cambridge, Mass.; repr. New York, 1963).

Greider, W. 1999. *Fortress America* (New York).

Grotowski, J. 1968. *Towards a Poor Theatre* (New York).

Hall, E. 1989. *Inventing the Barbarian: Greek Self-Definition through Tragedy* (Oxford).

Halliburton, D. 1988. 'Concealing Revealing: A Perspective on Greek Tragedy': 245-67 in *Post-Structuralist Classics*, ed. A. Benjamin (London).

Halliwell, S. 1998. *Aristotle's Poetics*. 2nd edn (Chicago).

Hardwick, L. 2000. *Translating Words, Translating Cultures* (London).

Havelock, E. 1957. *The Liberal Temper in Greek Politics* (New Haven).

———. 1982. *The Literate Revolution in Greece and Its Cultural Consequences* (Princeton).

Hegel, G.W.F. 1962. *Hegel On Tragedy*, ed. A. and H. Paolucci (New York, repr. 1975; orig. 1807-31).

Helbo, A., ed. 1991. *Approaching Theatre* (Bloomington).

Herington, J. 1985. *Poetry into Drama*, Sather Lectures vol. 49 (Berkeley).

Herman, E.S. 1982. *The Real Terror Network: Terrorism in Fact and Propaganda* (Boston).

Herman, E.S. and McChesney, R.W. 1997. *The Global Media: The New Missionaries of Corporate Capitalism* (London).

Herman, E.S. and O'Sullivan, G. 1989. *The 'Terrorism' Industry: The Experts and Institutions That Shape Our View of Terror* (New York).

Human Rights Watch. 1999. *The Enron Corporation: Corporate Complicity in Human Rights Violations* (New York).

Hutchinson, G.O., ed. and comm. 1985. *Aeschylus, Seven Against Thebes* (Oxford).

Izenour, G.C. 1977. *Theater Design* (New York).

Jebb, R.C., ed., comm. and tr. 1888. *Oedipus Tyrannus*, 2nd edn (Cambridge; repr. 1963).

Jones, J. 1962. *On Aristotle and Greek Tragedy* (London & New York).

Kant, I. 1998. *Critique of Pure Reason*, tr. and ed. P. Guyer and A.W. Wood (Cambridge; orig. 1781).

Kavanagh, J.H. 1995. 'Ideology': 306-20 in *Critical Terms for Literary Study*, ed. F. Lentricchia and T. McLaughlin, 2nd edn (Chicago)

Kemp, J.A. 1966. 'Professional Musicians in Ancient Greece', *Greece & Rome* 13:213-22.

Klare, M.T. 2001. *Resource Wars: The New Landscape of Global Conflict* (New York).

Knox, B.M.W. 1957. *Oedipus at Thebes* (New Haven).

———. 1979. *Word and Action: Essays on the Ancient Theater* (Baltimore).

Konstan, D. 2001. *Pity Transformed* (London).

Kosman, A. 1992. 'Acting: Drama as the Mimêsis of Praxis': 51-72 in Rorty 1992.

Lappé, M. and Bailey, B. 1998. *Against the Grain: Biotechnology and the Corporate Takeover of Your Food* (Monroe, Maine).

Lazenby, J.F. 1991. 'The Killing Zone': 87-109 in *Hoplites: the Classical Greek Battle Experience*, ed. V.D. Hanson (London).

———. 1993. *The Defence of Greece 490-479 BC* (Warminster).

Lebeck, A. 1971. *The Oresteia: A Study in Language and Structure* (Washington, DC).

Lemisch, J. 1975. *On Active Service in War and Peace: Politics and Ideology in the American Historical Profession* (Toronto).

Lesky, A. 1966. 'Decision and Responsibility in the Tragedy of Aeschylus'. *Journal of Hellenic Studies* 86:78-85.

Lessing, G.E. 1962. *Hamburg Dramaturgy*, tr. H. Zimmern (New York; orig. 1769).

Lévi-Strauss, C. 1963. *Structural Anthropology*, tr. C. Jacobson and B.G. Schoepf (New York; orig. 1958).

Ley, G. 1999. *From Mimesis to Interculturalism: Readings of Theatrical Theory Before and After 'Modernism'* (Exeter).

LIMC = *Lexicon Iconographicum Mythologiae Classicae* (Zurich & Munich, 1981-).

Lloyd, G.E.R. 1976. 'Views on time in Greek thought': 117-48 in *Cultures and Time*, ed. P. Ricoeur et al. (UNESCO: Paris).

Lloyd-Jones, H. 1982. *Blood for the Ghosts: Classical Influences in the Nineteenth and Twentieth Centuries* (Baltimore).

———, ed. and tr. 1996. *Sophocles, Fragments* (Cambridge, Mass.).

McAuley, G. 1999. *Space in Performance: Making Meaning in the Theatre* (Ann Arbor).

McChesney, R. 2000. *Rich Media, Poor Democracy: Communication Politics in Dubious Times* (New York).

McChesney, R., Wood, E.M. and Foster, J.B., ed. 1998. *Capitalism and the Information Age: The Political Economy of the Global Communication Revolution* (New York).

MacIntyre, A.C. 1981. *After Virtue: A Study in Moral Theory* (London & Notre Dame, In.)

Magdoff, F., Foster, J.B. and Buttel, F.H., ed. 2000. *Hungry for Profit: The Agribusiness Threat to Farmers, Food, and the Environment* (New York).

Mahajan, R. 2002. *The New Crusade: America's War on Terrorism* (New York).

March, J. 1998. *Cassell Dictionary of Classical Mythology* (London).

Mastronarde, D.J., ed. and comm. 1994. *Euripides, Phoenissae* (Cambridge).

Meiggs, R. 1972. *The Athenian Empire* (Oxford).

Mokhiber, R., and Weissman, R. 1999. *Corporate Predators: The Hunt for Mega-Profits and the Attack on Democracy* (Monroe, Maine).

Nagy, G. 1989. 'Early Greek Views of Poets and Poetry': 1-77 in *Cambridge History of Literary Criticism*, vol. I, ed. G.A. Kennedy (Cambridge).

———. 1996. *Poetry as Performance: Homer and Beyond* (Cambridge).

Nauck, A. and Snell, B., ed. 1964. *Tragicorum Graecorum Fragmenta* (Hildesheim).

Nehamas, A. 1992. 'Pity and Fear in the Rhetoric and the Poetics': 291-314 in Rorty.

———. 1999. *The Virtues of Authenticity: Essays on Plato and Socrates* (Princeton).

Nightingale, A.W. 1995. *Genres in Dialogue: Plato and the Construct of Philosophy* (Cambridge).

Nussbaum, M.C. 2001. *The Fragility of Goodness*, rev. edn (Cambridge).

Nuttall, A.D. 1996. *Why Does Tragedy Give Pleasure* (Oxford).

Ober, J. 1989. *Mass and Elite in Democratic Athens: Rhetoric, Ideology and the Power of the People* (Princeton).

Onians, R.B. 1951. *The Origins of European Thought About the Body, the Mind, the Soul, the World, Time, and Fate* (Cambridge).

Page, D.L. 1934. *Actors' Interpolations in Greek Tragedy* (Oxford).

Parke, H.W. 1977. *Festivals of the Athenians* (London & Ithaca).

Parker, A. and Sedgwick, E.K., ed. 1995. *Performativity and Performance* (New York).

Pelling, C., ed. 1990. *Characterization and Individuality in Greek Literature* (Oxford).

Phelan, P. and Lane, J., ed. 1998. *The Ends of Performance* (New York).

Pickard-Cambridge, A.W. 1968. *The Dramatic Festivals of Athens*, 2nd edn (Oxford; repr. with add. 1988).

Podlecki, A.J. 1966. *The Political Background of Aeschylean Tragedy* (Ann Arbor).

Poole, A. 1987. *Tragedy, Shakespeare and the Greek Example* (Oxford).

Prier, R.A. 1989. *Thauma Idesthai: The Phenomenology of Sight and Appearance in Archaic Greek* (Tallahassee).

Ranald, M.L. 1984. *The Eugene O'Neill Companion* (Westport, Conn.).

Rashid, A. 2000. *Taliban: Militant Islam, Oil and Fundamentalism in Central Asia* (New Haven).

RE = Real-Encyclopädie der classischen Altertumswissenschaft, 1893-1980, ed. A. Pauly and G. Wissowa (Stuttgart).

Redfield, J.M. 1994. *Nature and Culture in the Iliad: The Tragedy of Hector*, expanded edn (Durham, NC).

Rehm, R. 1994. *Marriage to Death: The Conflation of Wedding and Funeral Rituals in Greek Tragedy* (Princeton).

———. 2002. *The Play of Space: Spatial Transformation in Greek Tragedy* (Princeton).

Ricoeur, Paul. 1984. *Time and Narrative*, vol. 1, tr. K. McLaughlin and D. Pellauer (Chicago).

Ritz, D., ed. 2001. *Defying Corporations, Defining Democracy* (New York).

Rood, T. 1998. *Thucydides: Narrative and Explanation* (Oxford).

Rorty, A., ed. 1992. *Essays on Aristotle's Poetics* (Princeton).

Rose, P.W. 1992. *Sons of the Gods, Children of the Earth: Ideology and Literary Form in Ancient Greece* (Ithaca).

Rosenbloom, D. 1993. ' "Shouting Fire" in a Crowded Theater: Phrynichos' *Capture of Miletos* and the Politics of Fear in Early Attic Tragedy', *Philologus* 137:159-96.

Bibliography

St John Wilson, C. 1989. 'The Natural Imagination', *Architectural Review* 187:64-70.

Salkever, S. 1986. 'Tragedy and the Education of the Demos': 275-303 in *Greek Tragedy and Political Theory*, ed. P. Euben (Berkeley).

Sansone, D. 1975. *Aeschylean Metaphors for Intellectual Activity* (Wiesbaden).

Schechner, R. 1973. *Environmental Theater* (New York).

———. 1985. *Between Theater and Anthropology* (Philadelphia).

———. 1988. *Performance Theory* (London).

Seaford, R. 1994. *Reciprocity and Ritual: Homer and Tragedy in the Developing City-State* (Oxford).

Shepard, S. 1981. *Seven Plays* (New York).

Sifakis, G.M. 2002. 'Looking for the Actor's Art in Aristotle': 148-64 in Easterling and Hall.

Silverstein, K. 1998. *Washington on $10 Million A Day: How Lobbyists Plunder the Nation* (Monroe, Maine).

Smyth, H.W. and Lloyd-Jones, H., ed. and tr. 1957. *Aeschylus II* (Cambridge, Mass).

Sokal, A. and Bricmont, J. 1998. *Fashionable Nonsense: Postmodern Intellectuals' Abuse of Science* (New York).

Steiner, G. 1984. *Antigones* (Oxford).

Tallis, R. 1995. *Not Saussure: A Critique of Post-Saussurean Literary Theory*, 2nd edn (New York).

Taylor, C.C.W., tr. and comm. 1999. *The Atomists, Leucippus and Democritus: Fragments*. Phoenix supp. vol. 36 (Toronto).

Turner, V. 1969. *The Ritual Process: Structure and Anti-Structure* (London).

———. 1974. *Dramas, Fields, and Metaphors: Symbolic Action in Human Society* (Ithaca).

———. 1987. *The Anthropology of Performance* (New York).

Vernant, J.-P. 1972. 'Greek Tragedy: Problems of Interpretation': 273-95 in *The Structuralist Controversy*, ed. R. Macksey and E. Donato (Baltimore).

———, ed. 1995. *The Greeks*, tr. C. Lambert and T.L. Fagan (Chicago).

Vernant, J.-P. and Vidal-Naquet, P. 1988. *Myth and Tragedy in Ancient Greece*, tr. J. Lloyd (New York).

Waring, M. 1999. *Counting for Nothing: What Men Value and What Women are Worth*, 2nd edn (Toronto).

Webster, T.B.L. 1967. *The Tragedies of Euripides* (London).

West, M.L. 1992. *Ancient Greek Music* (Oxford).

Wiles, D. 2000. *Greek Theatre Performance: An Introduction* (Cambridge)

Williams, B. 1993. *Shame and Necessity*. Sather Lectures vol. 57 (Berkeley).

Wilson, E.O. 2002. *The Future of Life* (New York).

Winkler, J.J. and Zeitlin, F.I., ed. 1990. *Nothing to Do with Dionysos? Athenian Drama in Its Social Context* (Princeton).

Winnington-Ingram, R.P. 1980. *Sophocles: An Interpretation* (Cambridge).

———. 1983. *Studies in Aeschylus* (Cambridge).

Wycherley, R.E. 1962. *How the Greeks Built Cities*, 2nd edn (London).

———. 1978. *The Stones of Athens* (Princeton).

Yates, F.A. 1966. *The Art of Memory* (London & Chicago).

Bibliography

Zeitlin, F.I. 1990. 'Thebes: Theater of Self and Society in Athenian Drama': 130-67 in Winkler and Zeitlin.
———. 1996. *Playing the Other: Gender and Society in Classical Greek Literature* (Chicago).

Index